ASPECTS OF ACCRINGTON

ASPECTS *of* ACCRINGTON

Discovering Local History

Edited by

Susan Halstead & Catherine Duckworth

Series Editor
Brian Elliott

Wharncliffe Books

First Published in 2000 by
Wharncliffe Books
an imprint of
Pen and Sword Books Limited,
47 Church Street, Barnsley,
South Yorkshire. S70 2AS

For up-to-date information on other titles produced under the
Wharncliffe imprint, please telephone or write to:

> **Wharncliffe Books**
> **FREEPOST**
> **47 Church Street**
> **Barnsley**
> **South Yorkshire S70 2BR**
> **Telephone (24 hours): 01226 - 734555**

ISBN: 1-871647-65-7

A CIP catalogue record of this book is available from the
British Library

Cover illustration: Town Hall, Blackburn Road, Accrington

Printed in Great Britain by
Redwood Books, Trowbridge, Wiltshire

Contents

INTRODUCTION

by Susan A. Halstead and Catherine Duckworth

'Nostalgia is [the] wonderful emotion' which opens this first volume of *Aspects of Accrington*, which surveys not only the town of Accrington but also the district of Hyndburn. Looking at the past 'through rose-coloured glasses' is a pastime indulged by us all just as much as Harold Tootle with his childhood memories of growing up in the 1950s. Harry's reminiscences are of his play area of Huncoat; his memories, however, of bonfire nights long gone and working on hot summer days to earn extra pocket money will strike chords with many readers.

Harry's happy experiences of a golden era, when the threat of war had receded, contrasts sharply with those carefully researched by Jack Whittaker on the Boer War. Jack's involvement with the Church Lads' Brigade and knowledge of Brigade members who volunteered to serve in South Africa led him to search local newspapers for letters sent home to loved ones. An unusual perspective of wartime conditions is given in a vivid account of a violent storm endured by a ship laden with soldiers and horses.

Jack describes a yacht, originally bought as a wealthy businessman's plaything but later used as a hospital ship for injured soldiers, which also features in the article by George Randall. He traces the fascinating development of the Bullough dynasty from the birth of James in 1799 through the skills and activities of this inventive and entrepreneurial family to the worldwide success of the textile machinery manufacturers, Howard and Bullough. James' grandson built Kinloch Castle, a magnificent 'fairy-tale' castle on the Isle of Rum, which can be visited by us all as a monument to the imagination of our Accrington forbears.

The Bulloughs influenced not only industrial but also educational life in the town with their involvement in the formation of the Mechanics' Institution, which begins Bob Dobson's history of Accrington Grammar School. Humorous schoolboy memories mingle with affection for strict but respected teachers. Many of the old boys from the school grew up to be significant players on the national scene, part of Accrington's heritage which is as underestimated as its role at the centre of the Industrial Revolution.

The contribution made by one of Accrington's famous musical sons is finely documented by June Tomlinson in her study of Henry Watson who, like so many in this book, was influenced by life in a textile town. He did, however, develop the musical skills to take a music degree and was appointed a professor at the Royal Northern College of Music. His donation of books and music to Manchester Central Library ensured that his name would live on in the Henry Watson Music Library.

Another Henry, although of a very different character, is warmly recalled by June Huntingdon in her picture of 'an adventurous ancestor'. Henry Pilkington was described as a shawl printer when he married and he exported these skills to the USA. He was not afraid of the great unknown and survived many dangerous and exciting adventures, but he was successful enough to buy a large farm. He did, however, return home to his wife and child to establish Pilkington's Soap Works in Church. A colourful life indeed!

The sense of vision which took Henry to a foreign country was the same as that which inspired another local entrepreneur, Edmund Riley, to leave as his legacy the Victorian splendour of the Warner Street Arcade, one of the first shopping arcades in the country. Mike Booth helps us appreciate the story of the postal service from stagecoach deliveries to the opening of the magnificent new Post Office in this arcade to a time when the First World War placed additional strains on the delivery services.

Communication and textiles have played a significant role in the articles thus far, both of which are combined in Mike Clarke's detailed treatise on the Leeds & Liverpool Canal. He looks at the boat families who plied their trade in Altham with the growth of the coal mines and traces the development of the Enfield and Church areas, with the canal forming a vital link between productive industries and their markets.

The canal, once very much a way of life with families taking holidays on the working boats, is now part of the leisure industry. The workers of bygone days had fewer opportunities for leisure than today but this did not prevent an enthusiastic following for the ill-fated Accrington Stanley football team, whose misfortunes have ensured the name of Accrington remains in the national psyche. Jean Harrison describes not only the ups and downs on the football field but also the battles in the boardroom with the team's final, ignominious resignation from the Football League in 1962.

The crowds which originally supported Stanley also turned out to cheer their king in Helen Barrett's account of royal visits to the

Hyndburn area, commencing with that of George V in 1913. The pomp and circumstance of these occasions when prominent officials lined up to meet the monarch contrast with the enthusiastic welcome from flag-waving children for what was, in many cases, a very fleeting visit.

The most recent royal visitor, Prince Charles, applauded the environmental improvements at Foxhill Bank Nature Reserve, Oswaldtwistle, as does Charles Gidman in his introductory survey of the flora and fauna in Hyndburn. Contrasting the various forms of terrain from rugged moorland to more picturesque cloughs with their differing plant and animal species, Charles records the status of the local butterfly population, hitherto undocumented.

We would like to pay tribute here to all our contributors, some of whom have suffered difficult personal circumstances whilst working on their articles, but who have surmounted these with the conviction that documenting local history is of overwhelming importance and worthy of their endeavours. There are also many other dedicated local historians, whose research we have been unable to include in this edition, but they all play a vital role in recording the history of our community and educating future generations.

The theme of the remaining chapters can be summed up by the title, 'With injustice and oppression I make no compromise'. Catherine Duckworth tells the previously unsung story of Accrington's ground-breaking opposition to the imposition of Easter dues, effectively a religious poll tax imposed by the Church of England in the seventeenth century but resisted by the common man in 1860. Such another battle of right over wrong concludes our look at *Aspects of Accrington*. William Turner praises the extensive efforts made by local people to honour their dead not only of 'the war to end all wars', but also those of subsequent wars, as he describes the architectural details and unveiling ceremonies of all Hyndburn's civic war memorials. Nostalgia opened our look at Accrington's history and remembrance closes it. As we all look forward at the beginning of a new millennium, we must also look back, 'lest we forget'.

Anyone interested in making a contribution to *Aspects of Accrington 2* should, in the first instance, contact Susan Halstead and Catherine Duckworth, c/o Wharncliffe Publishing (Book Division) Limited, 47 Church Street, Barnsley S70 2AS enclosing a brief description of the proposed work.

1. THROUGH ROSE COLOURED GLASSES: LOOKING AT HUNCOAT

by Harold Tootle

NOSTALGIA IS A WONDERFUL EMOTION. It eases the heart with fond memories by allowing us to forget the harsh realities of life and look back to our younger days 'through rose coloured glasses'.

I have always considered that I was born into a blessed generation. I and all the other children who were born towards the outbreak of the Second World War have much to be thankful for. We had missed the terrible years of the great depression. Those harsh years of uncertainty and rationing during the war were little more than a game to us. We ran around the streets with a piece of wood for a gun, shooting Japs and Jerries.

When the war was over, our fathers returned from service abroad. Both my parents were working and there was good food on the table. It was in the summer of 1950 that my dad obtained work on the building of Huncoat Power Station (Figure 1) and we came to live in

Figure 1. Huncoat Power Station which opened 11 May 1956.
Lancashire County Council: Accrington Local Studies Library

Figure 2. The more rural surroundings of Huncoat. Looking towards the Coppice and the Hillock Vale area of Burnley Road from Woodside Road.
Lancashire County Council: Accrington Local Studies Library

the village. I was nine years old and Fred, my younger brother, was seven. After the long terraced streets of Blackburn and the back alleys for a playground, Huncoat was a child's paradise (Figure 2).

During that long summer holiday before starting at a new school, I had time to find new mates and explore the village. When the weather was fine we had Altham Clough for our adventures. We did, however, have to keep a wary eye open for the old fella, Sam, who lived at *Waterside*, a bungalow on the bank of the canal. If he saw us in the wood he would rant and rave, waving his stick in the air.

During those hot summer days we could earn a few bob haymaking. We would toil for hours in the fields raking the hay, with sandwiches for lunch and as much pop as we could drink. As an added incentive, we sometimes got a chance to drive the tractor. When we were not working on the farm, we spent our days at the broken bridge on the canal. This was situated halfway between Huncoat and Clayton-le-Moors and here the young folk from the surrounding area would congregate to go swimming. When swimming in the cut there was no need for a sun tan lotion, for there was always a thin film of oil floating on the surface! The coal barges would come chugging by, stirring up the mud, and we would have to wait for the water to clear. While we waited, many a lad and lass began their courting days by the broken bridge and some went on to marry and are still together to this day.

On the wet days, we would play in the old Perseverance Mill (Figure 3) at the bottom end of the village. This had been a spinning and weaving mill which had stopped production in 1941, but during the war it was used by the War Department for storage. On the railway siding by the side of the mill were some folding wooden boats which the army had used for river crossing. We had managed to open out one of the boats and, when covered with a canvas sheet, it made a terrific den; our gang spent many happy hours debating how to move the boat to the canal.

A large amount of material had been left behind when the mill had been cleared – thousands of yards of rubber pipes, aeroplane tyres and hundreds of tins of black, sticky 'Bostic'. There was also a room stacked from floor to ceiling with thick paper bags, which were used for lining packing cases. With all this fuel within two minutes walking distance, you can imagine what great bonfires we had. The fifth of November will never be the same again.

Figure 3. Perseverance Mill and Redac Brickworks, Huncoat as they were in 1898. *Lancashire County Council: Accrington Local Studies Library*

'Progging'[1] for the bonfire began at the end of September. We used to build the fire on the big back between Highbrake Terrace and the Redac brickyard, constructing a den inside and stacking the timber around it. The precious fuel had to be guarded against raids from the 'Sawdust City Gang', who would mount an attack from across the fields on the east side of Bolton Avenue.

'Sawdust City' or 'Toy Town', as it was also known, was an estate of pre-fabricated bungalows, constructed to ease the housing problems towards the end of the war and it housed workers employed at the Bristol Aircraft Factory at Clayton-le-Moors. It stretched from Burnley Road down the fields behind Saint Augustine's Church. Below this was a camp for some of the immigrant workers from Italy and Poland who had come over to work in the mines throughout the British coalfields (Figure 4).

Figure 4. A group of miners from Huncoat Colliery taken in the 1950s. The colliery closed on 10 February 1968. Do you recognise anyone behind the coal-dust? If so, please contact the staff in Accrington Local Studies Library.
Lancashire County Council: Accrington Local Studies Library

Figure 5. Huncoat Council School as it was in 1929. Harold Peel was head-master of the school from 1893 to 1931. *Lancashire County Council: Accrington Local Studies Library*

   With these workers had come the children with whom we tussled for supremacy. We would raid their bonfire and they would raid ours. This running battle would go on for weeks until the great night when we would visit our rivals' fire to see what was on offer. There would be roast spuds, baked in the fire, which had to be juggled from one hand to the other until they were cool enough to eat. Home-made spud pie was baked in the enamel washing-up bowl and home-made treacle toffee tasted better than any you could buy at Little Benny's shop on Station Road. At the end of the night we would head for home with a full belly, as black as the ace of spades and stinking of burnt wood and rubber.

   One of the village lads (who shall remain nameless for obvious reasons) decided to have a bonfire of his own. He would set fire to the mill, then run through the fields and up Bolton Avenue to watch the fire engine coming up Burnley Road. He enjoyed this so much he did it three times in one day!

   Over the wall in the Redac brickyard, about ten yards from the site

Figure 6. Huncoat Colliery 1953. New head gear at No 2 Shaft and rail wagons in forefront.
Lancashire County Council: Accrington Local Studies Library

of the bonfire was a huge stack of baled straw, which was used for packing bricks, and next to it was a fuel pump. For years there was no problem until the underground fuel tank ruptured and puddles of oil appeared on our side of the wall. After this we had to find another site for the bonfire.

Winter would now be closing in and we had to find somewhere to spend the wet, cold evenings. We spent two nights a week at the youth club which was held in the village school, still one of the best junior schools in Hyndburn (Figure 5). The rest of the week we had to fend for ourselves. There were a number of places we could hibernate, but both the mill and the boat were too cold. The waiting-room on the up-line of the railway station was ideal. There was always a coal fire roaring up the chimney and we could dim the gaslight to make it more cosy. We would have to keep the noise down or the porter would come across the line and run us off. One of the porters, little Jerry, was a tiny chap, not much over five feet tall but with the heart of a lion. He would hold the door and march us out in single file and attempt to give us a clip round the earhole as we dodged past him. One year, one of the older youths dropped a bundle of bangers down the station chimney and nearly gave the poor man a heart attack. After this there was no more waiting-room for us.

Along the railway siding at Huncoat colliery (Figure 6), was a long row of obsolete beehive coke kilns. With a little bit of ingenuity, one of these was converted into a den. A five-gallon oil drum and length of cast iron drainpipe for a chimney made a stove for the centre of the room. Fuel for the stove was two yards from the doorway on the railway wagons waiting to leave the colliery. One cold, wet night, a couple of the older boys with their girlfriends decided they would use our den for their courting. This was just not on. We climbed on top of the kiln. Passing round an empty tin can, we all contributed our own share of warm urine, poured it down the chimney and ran like hell! We were kept on the run for several days, avoiding the bigger lads until things calmed down.

Time passed and as we got older it was time to earn some extra money. I got a job delivering groceries for John Singleton at the post office and for this I had a big, black bike with a basket on the front. You'd be amazed how much that basket could hold! When full it felt like it weighed a ton. I would go into the back room to collect the groceries and my nostrils would be assailed by a multitude of aromas: smoked bacon, firelighters, soap, freshly ground coffee, and many other delights. The memory of them will stay with me for the rest of my days.

When the weather was fine so was the job. When the weather was bad, the job was also rough. I would put on an old army gas cape, pull down my cap and set off. Like the pony express the groceries had to get through! Four evenings a week and Saturday mornings, all for the princely sum of 7s 6d.

I delivered goods to all the outlying farms. At *Clough Side Farm* along the bank of the canal, an elderly lady, Mrs Imms, would always have a pot of tea and a piece of cake on the table when I arrived. To this day I still cannot fathom out how she knew to the minute when I would appear at the door. She had no phone and she could not see me approaching. On the other side of the coin was a lady who lived in one of those big houses on Whalley Road, not far from the hospital. She would empty the groceries onto the kitchen table and make me stand there and wait until she had checked them against her list. She would then dismiss me without so much as a thank you and certainly no tip. One particularly wet and miserable day, she complained that her order was damp and on the way out I rode the bike across the lawn leaving a two-inch deep track. Unlike the kindly Mrs Imms, this lady did have a telephone and she used it to good effect, so that when I returned to the shop there was hell to pay. The boss got me in the back room and gave me a real ear bashing. He said I should have covered the basket with my cape. Fat chance!

There were hard times as well as good, but that's another story. At the beginning of January 1956, I started at Bank Hall Colliery, Burnley with several other lads from the area to start training for work in the pit. The playing days were over.

Acknowledgements

I acknowledge with grateful thanks Lancashire County Council: Accrington Local Studies Library for kind permission to reproduce six photographs in this article.

Notes and References

[1] 'Progging' – a common term for the collecting of bonfire wood which seems to have been used only in the Huncoat area.

2. DESPATCHES FROM LOCAL LADS IN THE BOER WAR 1899-1902

by Jack Whittaker

THE SECOND ANGLO-BOER WAR, commonly known as the Boer War, was the culmination of increased tensions in southern Africa which had been building throughout the nineteenth century. Resentment in the population of Dutch descent, known as Boers or Afrikaners, against the British settlers, known as Uitlanders, heightened with the discovery of gold in Witwatersland and ownership of these rich deposits was fiercely contested. This ultimately led to the Boers declaring war on the British on 11 October 1899.

At first the Boers gained the upper hand defeating the new British army and besieging several major towns. In January 1900, General Frederick Sleigh Roberts became Commander-in-Chief of the British Forces and the besieged towns were gradually relieved. By June, when President Kruger had fled to Europe, Roberts believed the war had been won.

Guerrilla warfare against the occupying British troops, however, proved extremely successful and Kitchener, the new Commander-in-Chief, adopted a scorched earth policy, also herding non-combatants such as women and children into newly created concentration camps. Negotiations for peace culminated in the signing of the Treaty of Vereeriging in May 1902.

The death toll varies from source to source. In the concentration camps it was very high owing to disease and probably numbered between 20,000 and 40,000 people. Overall the British lost as many as 20,000 soldiers but the casualties for the Boers were much less, between 4,000 and 7,000 men. The number of African dead was not recorded. This article shows that there were also other casualties.

As we see in the final chapter, it was not until after the First World War that the names of those who died for their country were commemorated generally. The only local civic memorial to those who died in the Boer War is at Darwen, although there is a memorial in St James' Parish Church, Haslingden to the eleven men of the town who died in the war (Figure 1).

Very little information has been compiled about the local men, both regulars and reservists, who volunteered to go to the Boer War,

Figure 1. Memorial in St James' Parish Church, Haslingden to the memory of the eleven men from the town who died in the Boer War 1899-1902. It is made of white marble in the form of a scroll and was unveiled by the Mayor of Haslingden, 23 February 1904.

The cost of the memorial was raised by a committee of Haslingden ladies who, at first, intended the money to be spent on a hospital bed in South Africa for Haslingden soldiers. This was vetoed by the War Office so some of the money raised was spent on extra comforts for the troops there and the remainder set aside for the memorial.

William Turner 1995

nor about the men of the St John Ambulance Brigade who volunteered to serve at the front (Figure 2). In my childhood and youthful days, I knew quite a few of the men who went out to the Boer War and I have searched local newspapers to find letters sent home to loved ones waiting for news. Should these letters prove interesting to anyone researching their family or local history, as they have been to me in collating and compiling them, then I shall be amply compensated.

The first letter was from Sapper Hargreaves Ashworth and was published in the *Bacup Times* 25 November 1899. It paints a vivid yet gruesome picture of other casualties of the war.

En Route For The Transvaal

The following letter will probably be of interest to our readers, as it has been received from Mr Hargreaves Ashworth, a young man, formerly of the Royal Engineers en route for Cape Town. Writing on the 1 November from Canada Docks, Liverpool, he says,

'I only arrived in Liverpool this morning, and as we do not set sail till seven tomorrow morning, I will try to send this letter with the pilot when he leaves the ship, which is the SS Rapidan, *of over 7,000 tons, and only goes eleven knots an hour, so we shall not get in Cape Town under 28 days. We left Aldershot for Tilbury on 21 October, but as the Admiralty had over estimated the capacity of the ship, we were sent back to barracks to wait for this vessel.'*

Figure 2. Men of the St John Ambulance Brigade, ready for the Front. Taken for the *Accrington Observer and Times* after the arrival of the men in London, the photograph was published as a special supplement on Tuesday 6 February 1900.
Back row: Pte J. Lingard, Pte W. Britland, Pte T. Cottam, Pte G. Parkinson, Pte J. Taylor.
Front row: Pte T.H. Rawcliffe, Pte J.R. Woodcock, Sgt Rawcliffe, Pte W. Holden, Pte E. Dewhurst. Pte Grimshaw Parkinson was wounded during his service but recovered and also saw service in the First World War. *Lancashire County Council: Accrington Local Studies Library*

The letter is continued on 5 November (Sunday).

  'I started to write the above with the intention of sending it with the pilot when he left us but was too late, and since then we have passed the most horrible times imaginable.

  We left the river on Thursday at 7.00am and went down the Irish Sea, passing the Welsh coast in fine style, but as we were passing Lands End a gale arose blowing from the Atlantic. The Captain was *advised to go into some port, but he was firm and would not. All the time the wind and rain were sweeping the deck. We had 500 horses below, and as the ship rolled from side to side they went frantic, broke loose, and in a very short time were a mass of panting, seething, mangled animals. We were feeding them when it started and those who could extricate themselves from the mass of debris and animals and climb the upper deck did so. But some were less fortunate, and got kicked and trampled by the horses. One man had his ankle smashed, another his knee, one his arm, and several were bruised in different places. I managed to climb above by means of a cable, and when I got to the top I was almost swept away many times. The vessel was riding on its beam ends. We could do nothing but hang on and stare at each other with never a word.*

By this time we were in the Atlantic Ocean, when a stoker or fireman came gasping up with 'Fire! Fire! in the stoke hole'. We gave ourselves up for lost. One of the crew put the end of a cable in my hand and told me to rush along the deck with it, I did so, not knowing why. However I found we were dragging a pump and a hose along to the quarter deck, to get above the fire. After about an hour or so we managed to get it out, but to do so they had to put some of the fires out in the boiler. Then the engine broke down and in no time we were being tossed about like a cork. We got broadside on first on the top of a wave, then down in the hollow. The water seemed to touch the skies. Every man knew, or thought that he was lost. I wondered whether the vessel would go under first, or would the water cause the boiler to burst. But, at last they managed to get the other engine on and head the wind. Then we steered back for Liverpool, back through the gale. We lost two boats and the remainder were damaged. Then we went below to the horses. What a horrible bloody sight met our eyes. We found two men below, one in a fit, and the other mad. Since then we have thrown over 100 horses overboard, and the same number will have to be shot.

We are just outside Liverpool Docks. A boat with some reporters came alongside for news, but they would not give them any, only that we had lost a few horses, and been in a gale.'

The letter continues on 6 November.

Birkenhead Docks

'During last night we steamed into these docks for repair. The shipwrights are already on board and at work, and by the end of the week we shall no doubt be off again, and I hope we shall have a better voyage. For should I live to be 1,000 years old, I shall never forget that day. These are no sailors yarns, but the honest truth. They won't allow

us off the ship, and a good job too, or they would not get half of them back again'. The vessel referred to, the SS Rapidan is taking out a number of Royal Engineers and after repairs referred to, sailed for the second time from Birkenhead a week ago.'

The following was published in the *Accrington Observer and Times* of 9 February 1901.

Sgt A Kerr

If Mr James Kerr (Figure 3) *had been alive today he would have had reason to deplore the fate of a promising young nephew, Sgt James Alan Kerr, a son of Dr Kerr, of Edinburgh, formerly Her Majesty's Chief Inspector of Schools.*

Young Mr Kerr, he was but 26, joined the Scottish Sharpshooters as a trooper at the beginning of the war, and was afterwards promoted to a sergeant.

Like the brave man he was, finding his men in a tight corner in one of the many skirmishes with the Boers, he ordered them away and himself stayed behind, a target for a shower of bullets, until everybody else had found cover. He was wounded and after lying on the field in agony the long night through, was carried into camp with a broken leg, and after some days underwent an operation which ended fatally.

When his Colonel sent home the sad tidings he wrote this, 'I have lost the best young soldier and the best friend in the squadron.'

Sgt R. Fairclough

But that would not have been the only regrettable news for the folk at Dunkenhalgh, for in the list of Moddersfontein casualties published this week, there appears this:

'23rd Company Imperial Yeomanry:

2672 Sgt R. Fairclough, slightly wounded. Lance Kloof, near Sutherland 30 January.'

Figure 3. Mr and Mrs James Kerr of Dunkenhalgh. James Kerr was manager of the calico printing firm of F. Steiner and Co. He and his wife held the tenancy of Dunkenhalgh for some years from the Petre family and were at the forefront of local society. James Kerr died on 9 July 1892 and his wife survived him by only eight years, dying on 5 November 1900, aged 49. *Lancashire County Council: Accrington Local Studies Library*

That is a name the majority of people will recognise. Sergeant Fairclough was a relative of the late Mrs Kerr, and before joining the Yeomanry spent much of his time at Dunkenhalgh. A dashing young blade was 'Rowley' a nephew of the late Mrs Kerr, of Dunkenhalgh, and who is well known in the Accrington district, has received a commission in South Africa. He is now Lieutenant Fairclough, Prince of Wales Light Horse, Field Force South Africa. The regiment is a Welsh one of irregular horse, commanded by Colonel Owen-Thomas, one of the Welsh High Sheriffs.

Lieut Fairclough

Lieut Fairclough served for some years as an officer in the Church Artillery, and with the 11th Hussars in India, returning from that country in April 1899. On the call for Volunteers he joined the Blackburn troop of the Duke of Lancaster's Own Yeomanry, on the 4 January 1900, leaving for South Africa on the 10 February.

He took part in several engagements with the Boers, and was wounded in the left arm on the 24 January 1901, near Calvinia, Cape Colony, as a result he was sent to the Yeomanry Hospital at Maitland, Cape Town. He is now quite well again, and will join his new regiment at De Aar on the 26th inst, longing to have another 'little go' at the enemy. Many Observerites will be ready to congratulate Mr Fairclough on his recovery from his wound, and his promotion.

Another war item was published in the *Accrington Observer and Times* of the 9 February 1901.

A number of men of the Accrington and Clayton-le-Moors Volunteer Companies who have signified their willingness to go out to South Africa on active service went over to the Burnley headquarters on Sunday afternoon for medical examination.

The local men whose physical fitness satisfied Surgeon Capt Holt were, Privates Clegg, Cook, Greenwood, Harrison, Kenyon, Pilkington, Ryder, Rushton, and Walmsley.

Haslingden had on its pass list, Lieut Parker, and Privates Chew, Fitton, Nuttall, and Ratcliffe. The names of the men have been forwarded to the War Office, and orders are expected at any moment.[1]

George Bullough's Yacht. [George Bullough and his yacht appear again in the next chapter, ROUND THE GLOBE TO RUM: THE BULLOUGHS OF ACCRINGTON. Ed].

The Rhouma *is under the command of Captain R.J. Foxworthy, and carries a crew of thirty eight men all told* (Figure 4). *She is a* beautiful model of her class, and from a seaman's or yachtsman's stand-point her exterior is in keeping with her inner furnishings. All the latest navigating and steaming appliances which a builder or ship chandler could put on board, from her steering to her hose pipes, are of the latest and most approved pattern. She is fitted with a most compact set of triple expansion engines, supplied by Messrs Rawson and Co of Glasgow, while the vessel was built by Messrs Napier, Shanks, and Bell of Yorker, near Glasgow. On the voyage out several calls were made, the actual steaming time being 25 days and the mileage recorded on the log from Milford to Table Bay being 6,944.

Mr R. Mitchell, secretary to Mr George Bullough, who is at Cape Town in his steam yacht Rhouma, for the purpose of helping on the work of caring for convalescents, writes as follows to a friend in England:

'We had a good passage out here and commenced our work at Benguela, for at this place we picked up a Captain Quicke, 1st Dragoon Guards, who having started with a party of explorers under

Figure 4. George Bullough's yacht *Rhouma* moored in Table Bay, Cape Town. The raised wooden structure on the after deck is the ward. *George Randall Collection*

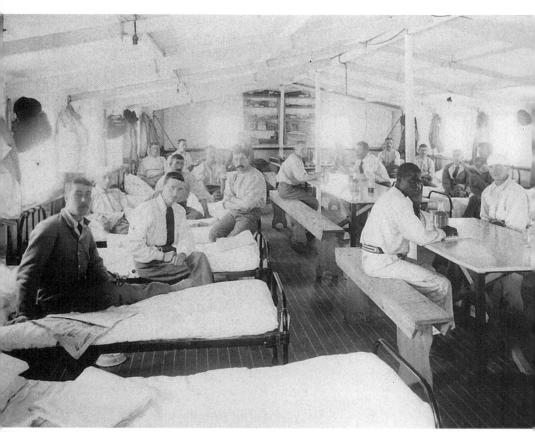

Figure 5. A view of the ward on board the *Rhouma*. Conditions here were light and airy, compared with the tents of the Portland and Rondebosch Hospitals. *George Randall Collection*

Figure 6. Portland Hospital, Bloemfontein, 1900. The tents which comprised the hospital were arranged in a large square. *Subscribers' Report from the Portland Hospital Committee.*

Major Gibbons, from the Zambesi, had made his way across the continent and landed at the above place with a black boy, the only one that came with him right across the continent. We had heard at Loanda that an expedition was expected to arrive somewhere on the west coast, and on inquiry at Benguela we found that a white man had arrived and was living 25 miles inland. We despatched a runner with an invitation to the man to come aboard and go on to South Africa. The result was that the man... worn to a shadow with fever and fatigue... appeared next day, and never shall I forget his first appearance on board. He was almost speechless with emotion at feeling himself really on board a British ship talking to Englishmen, and so I now have no hesitation in saying that the poor chap would have died if we had not come along. It appears he was living with some Boers until a ship should come along to take him to Loanda and thence on to Madeira and home. This family tried its best to prevent his coming with us, wanting to keep him so as to make money out of him, and in the event of his dying to seize his belongings. He had been sleeping in a room next to the donkey, and the vile smelling place was fast completing what the journey had begun, his dissolution. For two days on board he tried to bear up, but the fever kept devouring him, and when we arrived in Cape Town we got a doctor, who helped us to get him into a private hospital. He is still extremely weak, but the fever is getting less, and he is now able to take a little nourishment, and I firmly believe he is on the fair way to recovery. He wants to go back to the front very badly, but, poor fellow, he will take a year at least to pull around.

We have built a wooden structure on the large after-deck and have made a ward capable of holding twenty non-commissioned officers and men, with two bathrooms, a good lavatory, and wc (Figure 5). We are working in connection with the Portland Hospital (Figure 6), taking convalescents from them, and No 3 Army Hospital at Rondebosch. We have now twenty men and four officers aboard, and the people say we have the best ward in the colony. We are anchored in Table Bay about half a mile from the shore, and are most conveniently placed for the work. The Tommies are very delighted with their quarters, and it does one's heart good to see the poor fellows wounds healing up quickly under the influence of good plain food, rest and fresh air. Dr Bowlby, the chief of the Portland Hospital, says the men could not have a better place to recoup in. Singularly enough, there were some wounded men from the 2nd Worcesters in our first batch who had played football with our men in Bermuda, and were great chums with the crew on that account, and also two wounded

LIST OF PATIENTS — Steam Yacht "Rhouma," Cape Town, 1900.

No.	NAME.	OFFICIAL No.	REGIMENT.	DATE ENTRY.	DATE DISCHARGE	DISEASE.	REMARKS.
1	Private C. SMITH	3095	10th Hussars	4th March	13th March	Gun-shot wound on right thigh	
2	Private R. SPIERS	9414	2nd Coldstream Guards	" "	" "	Gun-shot wound on eye and neck	Bullet entered eye, down through palate, injured vocal cords, and broke collar bone
3	Private R. YACAMINI	3271	6th Inniskillen Dragoons	" "	20th "	Gun-shot wounds on right and left thighs	Flesh torn away badly with one-pounder shell
4	Private W. CHASE	5005	1st Essex Regiment	" "	" "	Gun-shot wound on left extremity	Bullet still remaining in leg
5	Private E. CAVENY	3616	12th Lancers	" "	14th "	Concussion of the brain	Lost sight of left eye
6	Private W. GIBBONS	8869	1st Coldstream Guards	" "	13th "	Ulcer	
7	Sergeant BANKS	4032	9th Lancers	" "	" "	Dysentery	
8	Private CALFF	4295	2nd Worcester Regiment	" "	" "	Gun-shot wound on leg	
9	Private E. C. WHANSTALL	4007	7th Inniskillen Dragoons	" "	" "	Gun-shot wound on foot	Bullet passed between first toes, under next two, and out between little toes
10	Private W. BUCKLE	4302	2nd Worcester Regiment	" "	17th "	Gun-shot wound on right thigh	
11	Private J. CUNNINGHAM	74	West Australian	" "	" "	Gun-shot wound on right thigh	
12	Private F. W. WALLACE	36	Victoria Mounted Rifles	" "	20th "	Gun-shot wounds on right and left thighs	Shot clean through both thighs while on horseback
13	Boy TEHANE	3229	King's Royal Rifles	" "	14th "	Conjunctivitis	Bugle boy
14	Private J. MASON	3514	East Surrey	" "	13th "	Gun-shot wound on foot	

LIST OF PATIENTS — Steam Yacht "Rhouma," Cape Town, 1900.

No.	NAME.	OFFICIAL No.	REGIMENT.	DATE ENTRY.	DATE DISCHARGE	DISEASE.	REMARKS.
15	Private W. COWDERY	3955	6th Inniskillen Dragoons	4th March	13th March	Gun-shot wound in thigh	
16	Private A. BUSBY	5371	East Surrey	" "	14th April	Gun-shot wound in hip	Also ingrowing toe nail
17	Sergeant J. H. P. BOND	6	New Zealand Mounted Infantry	" "	" "	Periostitis	
18	Corporal BURDETT	4320	12th Lancers	" "	17th "	Contusion	
19	Private A. MUNDY	3484	Oxford Light Infantry	" "	" "	Gun-shot wound in back	Bullet passed right through body
20	Private M'HUGH	4395	Scots Greys	" "	" "	Gun-shot wound in left forearm	
21	Private BLETCHLEY	3245	9th Lancers	13th March	29th "	Gun-shot wound in axilla	Bullet extracted
22	Corporal CLARKE	4436	1st Essex	" "	20th "	Gun-shot wound in throat	
23	2nd Corporal JACKSON	2296	Royal Engineers	" "	14th "	Rheumatism	Ulcer removed from back
24	Private T. STRANGE	6603	Gordon Highlanders	" "	22nd "	Dysentery	
25	Private E. HYLETT	5806	2nd Northampton	" "	" "	Sunstroke	
26	Private W. GAMBLE	35	Victoria Mounted Rifles	" "	2nd "	Gun-shot wound in shoulder	
27	Gunner NETTLESHIP	7321	Royal Horse Artillery	" "	22nd "	Contusion	
28	Private W. SHARPE	4749	1st West Riding	" "	20th "	Gun-shot wound in knee	

Figure 7. The first entries from the 'List of patients on board Hospital Ship SY *Rhouma*, Cape Town, 1900.' Two of the men from the 2nd Worcesters are listed, as is Boy Tehane, see Figure 9. The list does not include officers.

officers from the Worcesters (Figure 7).

The first man we met in Cape Town was G. who was up at Rum two years ago. He had come from Australia, joined the Kitchener's Horse, and in trying to break in a buckjumper, which had thrown the rough-rider twice, was pitched off and had his collar-bone badly broken. The day we met him he had just come out of the Portland Hospital, after a months residence therein, and so we carted him aboard, and he became next to Captain Quick, our first patient. A friend of ours - Dr Dixon - whom we knew when we were here before, has obtained leave of absence from his regular duties as chief doctor of the Loch Hospital, Cape Town, and has come to live on board and look after our patients. So I can fairly say we are complete now.

I am glad we came, because now we can see the good we do for the money expended, *whereas, if George* (Bullough) *had subscribed a big cheque to a fund, he would have had no chance of seeing the immediate effect of his gift.*

George (Bullough) *and I had a talk the other day, with the result that I have written to Jack Brown* (the factor at Rum) *to ask him to arrange and see how many convalescent officers they can put up in the new house at Rum, and also the* White House. *We want if possible, say about twenty. I have told Brown to see what he can do, and then put himself in communication with the authorities. If we can handle twenty men and six officers here, and say twenty officers at Rum, we feel that we are doing our little towards the great whole.*'

A further letter (undated) was received by Mr I. Walsh, Eagle Street, Accrington from his son Harry, who was in Cape Town. In the course of his letter he says:

I spent Monday night (apparently 5 March 1900) on board the Rhouma, *at the invitation of the Captain. They have now got the wounded on board, and they were having a concert. I never enjoyed a night better in my life. I am enclosing a cutting about the yacht. It is from the* Cape Argus *6 March 1900, and is as follows:*

Figure 8. A Portland ambulance.
Subscribers' Report from the Portland Hospital Committee

'The hospital camps in the Peninsula have been well chosen. The Wynberg and Rondebosch Hospitals are in ideal positions, and have been skilfully laid out, as the rapid recovery of our wounded heroes proves. In both camps the men are comfortable, and are of course, well attended (Figure 8). The military authorities have spared no pains to make these most complete, and every facility has been given by them to the public to help make the lot of the wounded ones as easy to bear as possible, and the privilege has been taken full advantage of. The public and private assistance has been immensely appreciated by the wounded officers and Tommies. The latest private offer in this way which has been made to and accepted by the military authorities is one which the patients whose privilege it is to come under it, appreciate most heartily. For the last week or so there have been lying at anchor in Table Bay two private steam-yachts. The owners of these pretty little crafts, doubtless drawn out here out of interest in the campaign, have quickly fallen to a sense of duty. The vessels are the Jason, a three-masted steamer owned by Mr Bibby of the Bibby Line of Steamships, and the Rhouma, owned by Mr Bullough.

Yesterday afternoon an Argus representative had the pleasure of inspecting the latter magnificent vessel, and witnessing how the wounded officers and men are provided for on the waters. The Rhouma has been converted into an ideal convalescent home. In ordinary circumstances this craft is a most luxuriously equipped vessel of 857 tons gross register - small as she undoubtedly looks compared with the huge liners at present lying in the anchorage. Her cabins and state rooms, which are furnished and upholstered in a most luxurious and up-to-date manner, have now been thrown open for the reception of wounded officers. Ample accommodation has been made for some fifteen of these, and more comfortable quarters could not be desired. The drawing-room and dining-room are magnificent specimens of the furnisher's art, while more comfortable state-rooms have certainly never been seen in Cape waters. On the upper deck a temporary hospital has been built for the wounded men, and every convenience has also been added, such as bathrooms, lavatories, etc. Twenty beds are in this ward, and ventilation, light, and comfort, which is the convalescents more immediate want, would compare with any sanatorium.

Mr George Bullough, who is on board his vessel, has not only placed his craft at the disposal of the authorities in this complete manner, but he is also to provide all the twenty men and fifteen officers with food, and the pantry is sufficient guarantee for that, comforts and medical attendance.

The men's quarters are already fully occupied and yesterday afternoon they looked extremely pleased with their new surroundings. Most of the men placed on board this vessel are of the class who have just so far recovered from very severe wounds as to be removed, and will yet require some considerable time and careful attention to reach complete recovery (Figure 9).

The fresh breezes of the bay - let us hope for no south-easters - will have a beneficial effect on the patients, while those who are fit for recreation and amusement shall have it provided. The Rhouma has on her davits a beautiful steam launch, and pleasant trips round the large fleet of transports will be made, while music and other evening pastimes will not be neglected.

The Rhouma is in fact, an ideal resting place away out from all the hurly-burly, to those men who have so recently come through so many trying times of endurance, and it is to be hoped that the splendid effort of Mr George Bullough, which has been made at some considerable expense and self-sacrifice will be the means of returning to strength so many of those for whom it is intended. The Rhouma will be thrown open to friends of the patients every Tuesday

Figure 9. Two of the patients. The one on the left probably Boy Tehane, bugle boy no 3229 with the Kin Royal Rifles. He was discharged on 14 March havi recovered from conjunctivitis. The other patient unknown. *George Randall Collection*

and Friday afternoon from three until five.'

A list of the patients received on board the *Rhouma* in the year 1900 was found in the library at *Kinloch Castle*. A copy was kindly presented to Accrington Library's Local Studies Department by George W. Randall, of the Kinloch Castle Friends Association. The list includes the name, rank, number and regiment of each soldier, the date he was received on board the *Rhouma* and the date on which he was discharged from the latter; also remarks and the disease or wounds the patient had suffered and the name of the place where the patient was wounded.

Prior to spending a few weeks' convalescence on board the *Rhouma*, a total of 181 patients were treated at Portland Hospital, No 3 General Hospital and Wynberg Hospital before being received on board at different intervals.

The *Rhouma* sailed home in October 1900, with a complement of convalescent soldiers who became the first occupants of the recently completed *Kinloch Castle* on the Isle of Rum. For this act of patriotic devotion, George Bullough was knighted in December 1901 at the age of 31 years.

The Boer War was reported in depth in the local papers with accounts of the action as each week went by and including, as has been seen, first hand reports of the hardships suffered by the soldiers and others. This was soon to be eclipsed by the events of the Great War, but I hope that those who fought and fell so far from home during the Boer War will also be remembered.

Notes and References

1. Lieut, later Captain, Parker and Private Chew are also commemorated on the memorial in Haslingden Church, see Figure 1.

3. ROUND THE GLOBE TO RUM: THE BULLOUGHS OF ACCRINGTON

by George W. Randall

MOST PEOPLE HAVE HEARD of the Lancashire town of Accrington if only because of its football team, Accrington Stanley [whose story is documented in Chapter 9. Ed]. Many people in Accrington will remember the Globe Works of Howard and Bullough Ltd, cotton machinery manufacturers. Not so many have heard of the Scottish Island of Rum or are aware of its link with the company, the Bullough family and the town.

Rum lies just south of the Isle of Skye, off the west coast of Scotland. The island was bought in 1886 by John Bullough and was inherited in 1891 by his son George, who six years later commissioned a dream castle to be built at the coastal township of Kinloch. In 1957 Lady Monica Bullough, widow of Sir George, sold the island to the British nation under the auspices of the then Nature Conservancy Council for £23,000. The writ of conveyance stipulated that Rum had to be 'used as a nature reserve in perpetuity and *Kinloch Castle* maintained as far as may be practicable'. Today the island ranks as a World Heritage Site, a Biosphere Reserve and an Area for the Special Protection of Birds. *Kinloch Castle*, part of which is used as hostel accommodation, survives as a fully furnished time capsule of the Edwardian era and the whole is in the care of Scottish Natural Heritage, a government agency responsible to the Scottish Parliament (Figure 1).

The Bullough family can trace their ancestry back in Lancashire to c1200, when Stephen Bulhalgh held land in Kirkdale, County Lancaster. His son, Henry, of Fazakerley, Walton and Kirkdale, County Lancaster, received a grant of land at Walton and Walston Wood at the end of the thirteenth century. The estate then passed to Henry's son, Robert, in 1321. Robert Bulhalgh had three sons, William, Richard and Thomas, and it is from the latter that the Bulloughs of Accrington are thought to descend. Ten generations later, Bulhalgh to de Bulhalgh, Bulhaigh, Bulhaighe, Bulowghe and finally, around 1580, the first known Bullough was born at Little Hulton, Parish of Dean, County of Lancashire. Another seven generations passed until, in 1799 at Deane, Westhoughton, James and Anne Bullough had a son they named James, who was destined

Figure 1. *Kinloch Castle* from Loch Scresort. *Author's collection*

to become co-founder of Howard and Bullough Ltd, Globe Works, cotton machinery manufacturers, Accrington.

James Bullough was a hard worker, a mechanical genius, who by the age of seven was working as a handloom weaver, before the power-loom and when steam was very much in its infancy. The potential of steam power, the demise of the cottage industry, the rapid rise of factories as centres of employment and the subsequent population growth in towns and cities were just around the corner.

The inhabitants of Accrington in the early 1800s numbered under 3,500, principally involved in handloom weaving. Five small spinning mills existed, worked by water power. Light was from oil lamps or candles and travel was on foot, horse-back or by stagecoach. New and improved machines began to make an appearance but were strongly resisted, as mill operatives feared loss of work. The year 1812 saw Luddite riots in Lancashire and Yorkshire. Employers eventually realised the damaging effects on their businesses from better equipped competitors if they did not respond to change and, by 1818, the first power looms were being introduced into Lancashire's mills. Against this background, James Bullough, still only in his teens, worked tirelessly on new ideas and ways which would improve machine efficiency. By the ingenious use of a twisted hair connected to a bell, he invented and utilised for his own loom a simple device which informed him when the cross yarn, or weft, was broken. This became known as the Self-acting Temple. In 1824, while employed as an overlooker at factories in Bolton and Bury, James married Martha Smith with whom he had four daughters and three sons during their 46 years of marriage. The following year he became manager of a small factory where he introduced the Dandy Loom, an improved hand-loom. By 1826 James Bullough was employed as overlooker at Rodgett's Cotton Mill, Preston. This was the year of the Power Loom Riots when the populace was suffering great distress as a result of the lack of factory orders, rising costs of living and unemployment for which the power looms were blamed. The whole area was engulfed in serious unrest requiring the swearing in of special constables and use of the military, which resulted in ten people being transported for life and thirty more receiving prison sentences of between three and eighteen months. Further riots broke out in 1829 in which several people lost their lives.

Whilst at Preston, James Bullough met William Kenworthy. The latter became associated with Brookhouse Mills at Blackburn and persuaded Bullough to join him as tackler. Experimentation and invention continued and 1841 was a year which revolutionised the weaving trade with the joint patenting of two inventions, the Roller Temple and Weft Fork for power looms. A great depression was again hanging over the industry, which was not conducive to the ready acceptance of new machines or ideas. Employers were urged by their workers to have nothing to do with the 'professed improvement of the loom, introduced at the Brookhouse establishment'. Disturbances broke out and 700 Special Constables were called up as protesters went from mill to mill and town to town knocking the boiler plugs out of the machines, thereby putting them out of action. For a while James Bullough was forced to leave Blackburn, returning after opposition calmed down. History records the period as the Plug-Drawing Riots of August 1842. In 1844 he invented the Loose Reed, which greatly increased the speed of the loom and reduced damage to the cloth; it formed the basis of many subsequent improvements. In 1845, after fifteen years at Brookhouse, James Bullough left, creating a new partnership with two other former employees, Robert Watson and John Fish; together they took over the cotton business at Stone Bridge Mill, Oswaldtwistle.

Within a short time a new venture, which was to last almost five

Figure 2. Shoe Mill, Baxenden. *Lancashire County Council: Accrington Local Studies Library*

Figure 3. James Bullough, from a portrait which hangs in the dining room at *Kinloch Castle*. *Author's collection*

years, began in conjunction with his cousin, Adam Bullough, at Waterside, near Darwen. Around 1850 James Bullough moved to Baxenden where, trading as James Bullough and Son, he took over Shoe Mill below Hill Street; a 70-strong workforce operated 75 looms in this refurbished loom shop, with its carding, twisting and spinning floors (Figure 2). Later, Victoria Mill Weaving Shed, also at Baxenden, was acquired and operated by James Bullough junior. With two of his three sons now old enough to help run the various business interests and the youngest, John, completing his education, James senior (Figure 3), returned to what he liked doing best, inventing and devising ways of improving machinery. In 1852 with two of his weaver employees, David Whittaker and John Walmsley, he took out a patent on 'an improved sizing machine', known as the Slasher, which was to lead to a milestone in the life of the Bulloughs and the town of Accrington.

In 1853 John Howard, a 38 year old engineer from Bury (Figure 4), chose Accrington as the site for a loom making business in partnership with James Bleakley. The enterprise was small, four employees in a cluster of wooden huts. There seems to be no record of why Bleakley withdrew from the venture taking with him the working capital, but John Howard persevered and, in 1856, he and James Bullough joined forces to form Howard and Bullough, Globe Works, Accrington. A condition of the partnership was that John Bullough joined the company, which he did in 1862 at the age of 25, assuming control of the business following the deaths of John Howard in 1866 and his father on 31 July 1868. James Bullough is interred in the family vault at Christ Church, Accrington, along with his wife, son James, daughters Lucinda and Jane and Jane's husband,

Figure 4. John Howard. *Lancashire County Council: Accrington Local Studies Library*

Alexander Grierson. Inside the church is a fine memorial window to James and Martha Bullough.

John Bullough (Figure 5), at only 31 years old, was now responsible for the future of Globe Works, where the full time production of cotton spinning and manufacturing machinery had commenced in the early 1860s and which now employed a workforce of 500. Unlike his father, he was ebullient and extrovert. He

Figure 5. John Bullough, also from a portrait hanging in the dining room at *Kinloch Castle*. *Author's collection*

benefited from a good education, having attended Queenswood College in Hampshire, an exceptional and early centre of scientific learning. At Glasgow University, where he studied Arts, he developed an appreciation for literature and music. Like his father, he had a brilliant mind for invention and a shrewd sense for commerce, coupled with great managerial skill.

The firm began to grow and, in 1876, John Bullough crossed the Atlantic to visit the American Exhibition, where he spotted a spindle which made the ring spinning of yarn practical by doubling the spinning speeds. He immediately recognised the potential of its application to Howard and Bullough's business and offered the American inventor, F.J. Rabbeth, a considerable sum of money for the patent. After some deliberation, Mr Rabbeth sold the rights to John Bullough and a Rabbeth Frame was shipped to Accrington along with the necessary machine tools and equipment for its manufacture.

In 1878, the manufacture of the Rabbeth Ring Spindle commenced at Globe Works and its success spurred a massive extension and reconstruction programme, including moulding shops and timber yards. New and larger engine houses, a dozen in all, were required to drive ever more machinery as production increased and the workforce grew to over 2,000. Within a few years, many millions had been produced for the home and world market, turning Globe

Figure 6. *Rhyddings Hall*, Oswaldtwistle. *Lancashire County Council: Accrington Local Studies Library*

Works into the truly global empire its name implies.

John Bullough married Bertha Schmidlin, the daughter of a Swiss cotton manufacturer from Thun, near Berne, on 1 February 1869 at the English Church, Brienz, near Thun. A son, George, was born the following year and a daughter, named after her mother, was born on 8 April 1872 at the family home, The Laund, Accrington and christened at Christ Church, Accrington. The family moved to *Rhyddings Hall,* Oswaldtwistle a few years later (Figure 6). John Bullough was by now an extremely wealthy man and gave generously to many local good causes, including the local cricket, swimming and football clubs, being president of the latter until his death. He established his company's Technical School for the furtherance of employee skills, helped found the Accrington Mechanics' Institution [see also Chapter 11, ACCRINGTON GRAMMAR SCHOOL ACCLAIMED. Ed] and, as an enthusiastic supporter of the Conservative and Unionist Party, contributed to the building of the Conservative Club itself, later becoming chairman. Selected to stand for Parliament, he later withdrew on the grounds of business commitments. He was appointed a magistrate of the Accrington Borough in 1880, but never took his seat. His exuberant character and strongly held opinions, which he was only too willing to share and defend, made him a much sought after and widely reported speaker.

Accrington Town Hall, St Peter's School, Accrington and Church Industrial Co-operative Society, the local Primrose League and the Conservative Club were just some of the many platforms from which John Bullough delivered his speeches on topics ranging from, 'Why a working man should be a Conservative', 'Mr Chamberlain and the land question', 'Licensed victuallers v teetotalers' to 'Thoughts on the Irish question'.[1]

John Bullough loved Scotland. In 1879, he rented the shooting rights on the island of Rum from his great Conservative idol, the Marquis of Salisbury, and in 1884 purchased the 50 square mile Meggernie Estate with its sixteenth century castle in the upper reaches of Glen Lyon, Perthshire. It was the ideal retreat. For seventeen years, his enormous driving force, business prowess and exceptional inventive skills had ensured the successful growth of Howard and Bullough but he was quick to identify similar attributes in others and they became his managers. Whether this single minded devotion to work was instrumental in the break-up of the union with his wife we can only speculate. With the purchase of his highland home came his second marriage, held at *Meggernie Castle* on 8 September 1884 to Alexandria (Alec) Marian Mackenzie, the daughter of a prominent banker in Stornoway, Isle of Lewis. She was much younger than her 44 year old husband, whose son, George, at this time was fourteen and his daughter, Bertha, twelve. John and Alec Bullough had two children. Their son, John, was born on 13 February 1886 and became popularly known as Ion. A daughter, Gladys, was born two years later.

The Bullough home at *Rhyddings Hall*, Oswaldtwistle, was leased from Robert Watson, a former partner of James Bullough in 1845 and now a highly successful mill owner in his own right. However, John's heart was in the Scottish highlands and he gradually spent more and more time at his Perthshire estate and visiting the island of Rum. On 5 June 1886, *The Times* advertised:

> *Island of Rum. Magnificent Sporting Island on the West Coast of Scotland for Sale... By Auction...*

The 26,000 acre island was bought by John Bullough for £35,000, equivalent to about £2.1 million today.

John Bullough was not neglecting his business during this time. Between 1868 and 1888 he took out 26 patents in his own name and was joint patentee on many more. He master-minded expansion after expansion, creating hundreds of extra jobs, as Howard and Bullough became the largest manufacturers of ring spinning frames and ring weft frames in the world, machines they perfected with the personal assistance of Mr Rabbeth, the inventor of the spindles and rings. Their new patent revolving flat carding engine could 'be adjusted to the thousandth part of an inch by the most ordinary workman', whilst their slubbing, intermediate and roving frames boasted Electric Stop Motion. Seventy five per cent of production went overseas, to Europe, the Far East, Canada, the USA and Brazil, countries where the company was involved in setting up cotton mills bearing its stamp.

Taking advantage of his choice of first class managers to run his business, John Bullough spent more and more time on his Scottish estates, especially the Isle of Rum. Unfortunately, his time to enjoy the fruits of his labours was short lived. Dedication to his commercial interests had slowly undermined his health, which grew steadily worse and early in 1891, suffering a slight lung infection, he set off with his wife and their two children for a few weeks at Monte Carlo, hoping that the warmer Mediterranean climate would restore his health. They planned to be back in Accrington to join the celebrations for his son George's coming of age on 28 February. By the time they arrived in a fog cloaked London, John Bullough's condition had deteriorated, congestion of the lungs set in and, with his family at his bedside, he died on 25 February 1891. He was 53. When the sad news reached Accrington, flags were flown at half-mast on public and private buildings as a token of the town's deep respect for a true 'man of mark' and captain of Accrington industry.[2]

The Bullough family had hoped for a quiet funeral but, as a measure of the esteem in which Mr Bullough had been held, thousands turned out to pay their respects. Howard and Bullough's workforce represented half the homes in Accrington. The train from London, with a special coach for Mrs Bullough, the two young children and her husband's coffin, arrived in Accrington at 4.25pm on 27 February. Members of the family were awaiting their arrival and John Bullough's twenty year old son, George, assisted his step-mother from the carriage onto the platform. The station was crowded with citizens who had paid one penny, the fare to the nearest destination, to gain access. The coffin was carried from the train to the hearse by foremen from Howard and Bullough. The entourage, with the Primrose Reed Band, Accrington Corporation Fire Brigade and Globe Works Fire Brigade in full uniform, then proceeded past the new Conservative Club, along streets lined with townspeople all wishing to express their personal last respects, to Christ Church, where the vicar, the Reverend Greensill, preached the memorial sermon. His text was from St Luke, chapter 12, verse 40: 'Be ye therefore ready also; for the Son of Man cometh at an hour when ye think not'.

The church was filled with 1,600 people with many hundreds standing outside. Reverend Greensill endeavoured to reassure his congregation, on whose faces he detected some anxiety as regards the future, that John Bullough had trained his workforce well and surrounded himself with managers of the highest calibre in order to carry the business forward. He reminded them of the words of the hymn they had just sung, 'O God our help in ages past, Our hope for years to come...'. Prayers were said for the deceased, his business and its 2,250 workforce. Special supplication was made for Mrs Bullough, her three year old daughter Gladys and son Ion, who had celebrated his fifth birthday two weeks earlier. After the last hymn, *'Just as I am'*, and with the organist playing *'The Dead March'*, John Bullough's coffin was placed in the family vault at Christ Church alongside the remains of his mother and father.

In his will, made only three months before his death, John Bullough left a personal fortune of £1,091,835 net, equivalent today to about £68 million, his two Highland properties and his

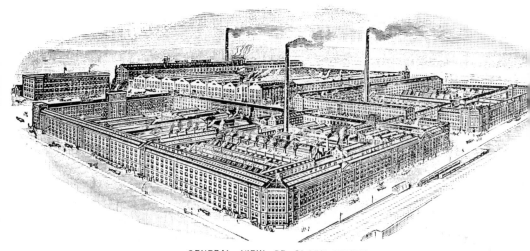

HOWARD & BULLOUGH, LIMITED, ACCRINGTON.

GENERAL VIEW OF GLOBE WORKS.

Founded in 1853. Now occupying, with Extensions. a total floor area of 51 95 acres (210,240 square metres).

Figure 7. Globe Works, Accrington, from an advertisement feature in Machinery Calculations, 1925. *Lancashire County Council: Accrington Local Studies Library*

possessions in Accrington. He instructed that Howard and Bullough be sold or converted into a limited liability company; the latter option prevailed. Provision was made for his widow who, in 1892, married Lt-Col John Robert Beech and for his daughters, Bertha and Gladys. His five year old son, Ion, was to inherit *Meggernie Castle* and estate plus half the share capital in Howard and Bullough upon his majority. Elder son, George, received the other 50 per cent interest in the business, the Isle of Rum Estate and the 55 foot, 24 ton cutter, *Mystery*, which had only been purchased the previous year to aid the ferry service to Rum.

On 28 February 1891, the day after his father's funeral, it was George Bullough's twenty first birthday; it must have been a very sad period in his life. Educated at Harrow School and now a cavalry officer, he had spent time at Globe Works, learning the business from the ground floor up, where he was well-known and liked amongst the workforce. His uncle, Tom Bullough, was chairman, a position he retained until his retirement in 1904, when he was succeeded by his nephew.[3] In 1891, Howard and Bullough was converted into a private limited company, backed by George Bullough as the major shareholder. Three years later due to ever-increasing growth, it was turned into a public company with assets of £750,000. Within a few years, owing to continued success, it became necessary to increase shareholders' interests, by the capitalisation of reserves, to £1,250,000, equivalent to £75 million today. In 1893 the Howard and Bullough American Machine Company was established at Pawtucket, Rhode Island, to take advantage of the huge and lucrative American market. The company continued to expand and, at its zenith in the mid-1920s, Globe Works employed almost 6,000 people, with a floor area of 52 acres or 210,240 square metres! (Figure 7). The running of the business continued in the tried and trusted hands of its directors and senior managers, including Mr S. Tweedale, who had overseen the introduction of the Rabbeth Spindle from the United States, and Mr J. Smalley, co-inventor with John Bullough of the Electric Stop-motion, which has been of great importance to a variety of machines.[4]

Figure 8. George Bullough as a young man. *Author's collection.*

George Bullough was dark, handsome, six feet five inches tall and loved all sport, particularly horse riding (Figure 8). He was now immensely rich, owned the magnificent Island of Rum, a yacht and enjoyed an annual income from his shareholding in Howard and Bullough Ltd in excess of £300,000, equivalent to about £1.8 million today. One of his first acts was to re-inter his father on Rum, the island he had loved so much. He had a mosaic lined, groin vault built into a hillside at the old township of Harris, but after some unkind remarks by visitors, likening it to a subterranean Victorian lavatory, George had a Doric style mausoleum erected nearby and his father was finally laid to rest in a central, sandstone sarcophagus. Upon their respective deaths, Sir

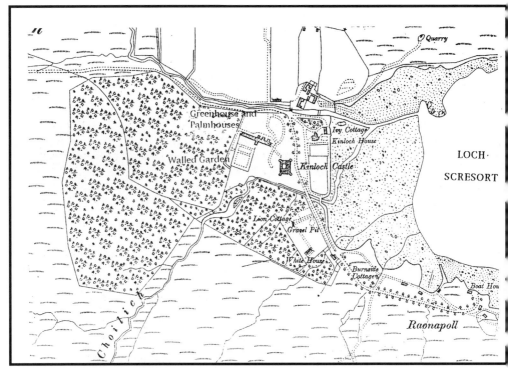

Figure 9. Enlarged extract from Ordnance Survey map (1:10560) 1877, revised 1898, showing *Kinloch Castle*, which at the time would be under construction. The extensive glasshouses and walled gardens are already shown to the left of the castle. No conservatory is marked. Note Kinloch House, built in the late 1820s by Dr Lachlan Maclean, and home to the island laird up to the building of *Kinloch Castle*. *Author's Collection.*

George and Lady Bullough would also be entombed at Harris, one on either side of John Bullough.[5] This deed done, George Bullough set about enjoying his wealth.

Travel to Rum was not easy, with no regular ferry service and always at the mercy of the weather. Even owning a boat made the journey little more certain. However, an ocean-going vessel could provide travel in the height of luxury, anywhere, anytime. In 1895 George Bullough made his first major purchase, the 670 ton, twin decked, steam yacht *Maria* which he renamed, *Rhouma*. She had been built in 1893 at the Glasgow yard of Napier, Shanks and Bell with a length of 221 feet and a breadth of 28 feet. Once on the island, accommodation was most unsatisfactory. *Kinloch House* by the foreshore, which had been used by the laird since being built 70 years earlier, was small, rat infested, and totally unsuitable for a young gentleman. George wanted an impressive mansion so, in 1897, the foundation stone was laid for *Kinloch Castle*, a four square, castellated, two storey hunting lodge, designed by London architects, Leeming and Leeming (Figure 9).

For three years kilted workmen, many from the Accrington area, laboured sometimes by candlelight to build the red sandstone edifice around a central courtyard, with a glazed verandah walkway to three sides. An imposing off-centre, square entrance tower with round turret, facing east across Loch Scresort to the Scottish mainland, would have been the first glimpse of this £250,000 (equal to £15 million today) dream home, as the steam yacht *Rhouma* rounded the headland on arrival at Rum (Figure 10).

Figure 10. Water colour by Byron Cooper. *Kinloch Castle* from the shores of Loch Scresort. Byron Cooper was commissioned by Sir George to paint scenes of the island. Many examples of his work are on display in the castle, showing what it was like before the trees grew. Note the conservatory and palm houses, to be seen on either side of the castle. *Author's collection*

While all this work was proceeding, George Bullough, still only in his late twenties, sailed the world in his yacht. Twenty photographic albums, containing 800 black and white and several hand coloured photographs, record his travels during the closing years of the nineteenth century around South Africa, China, Australia, New Zealand, California, India, Burma, Japan and the Pacific islands;[6] this was a good time to pick up a few choice and unusual items for his new island home. Magnificent oriental vases, bronze sculptures, screens and furnishings were stowed away on board *Rhouma*.

The autumn of 1899 brought the yacht to Table Bay, Cape Town, carrying recruits from Great Britain for the Boer War which broke out on Wednesday 11 October. George Bullough immediately placed *Rhouma* at the disposal of Queen Victoria's forces for use as a hospital ship and recruiting station, as already detailed in Chapter 2, DESPATCHES FROM LOCAL LADS IN THE BOER WAR. A framed canvas deck-house was erected as a twenty bed ward. Bedsteads, bedding, water tanks, baths and all food items were provided by George

Figure 11. View of *Kinloch Castle* as it is today. The glazed verandah has been repaired, but the conservatories, palm houses and extensive pleasure gardens are long gone. The trees have grown to form a magnificent backcloth topped by the Rum Cuillins. *Author's collection*

Bullough. Two members of his crew were sent to assist the army staff at the nearby Rondebosch Hospital. Other members of the *Rhouma's* company helped entertain the patients on board with deck games, music, stories and fishing. During the twelve months the yacht remained in Table Bay, 216 men and 46 officers were treated on board with no fatalities. One year later, *Rhouma* sailed home to Scotland with a complement of convalescent soldiers who became the first visitors to the now completed *Kinloch Castle*. On 11 December 1901, George Bullough was created a Knight Bachelor by King Edward VII on behalf of a grateful nation for his patriotism, which had helped alleviate so much pain and suffering amongst British troops.

From completion to 1914 were golden years in the history of *Kinloch Castle* (Figure 11). Sir George Bullough was immensely proud of his new island home. Designed as a military officer's 'bachelor pad', it incorporated the latest technological innovations: hydro-electric light, from electrical engineers, G.H. Woods & Company, Blackburn, Lancashire; telephone; double glazing; air conditioning; central heating; hot and cold running water; and superb bath cabinets (Figure 12), which even at the end of the twentieth century are something to behold and experience! Musical entertainment was provided by a pneumatically-operated instrument known as the *Orchestrion* (Figure 13). The rendition, generated via a punched paper roll to a series of trumpets, pipes and drums, was

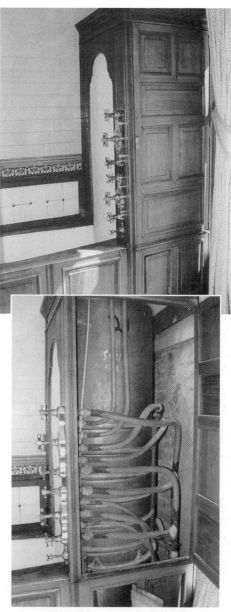

Figures 12a and b. The bath cabinet in Lady Bullough's bathroom. The water can spray, douche or wave from above, below or the sides. *Author's collection*

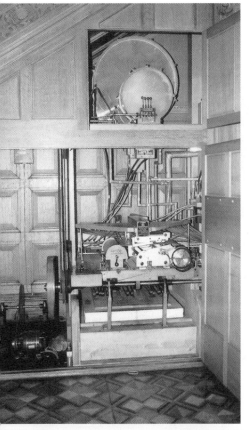

similar to a large band in full swing. In addition there was a magnificent ballroom with fully sprung floor, huge Waterford crystal chandelier and minstrel's gallery. Outside were a tennis court, golf course and bowling lawn. There was also an indoor raquette ball court, which still exists. To this incredible home he invited his friends, some of whose names are recorded in the three *Rum Forest Game Books*.

In October 1902, the guests included the Marquis de la Pasture,

Figure 13. The Orchestrion, originally ordered for Queen Victoria who died before its delivery, was fitted into the space below the stairs of the Hall. The instrument still plays, its notes reverberating around the castle. *Author's collection*

Figure 14. Lady Bullough's drawing room. The walls are covered in hand embroidered silk; the silk damask covered chairs are swathed in original dust covers as though awaiting the next visit of the family. *Author's collection*

Figure 15. Mahogany fitted and panelled dining room, which contains the portraits of James, Martha and John Bullough and a Byron Cooper water-colour. *Author's collection*

Figure 16. The hall opens to two storeys and is the main entrance to the castle. The portraits of Sir George and Lady Bullough with which they marked each other's fortieth birthday hang one above the other. The hall is filled with bronze sculptures, oriental vases, furniture and other choice items which Sir George brought back from his world cruises. *Stephen Frankland*

accompanied by his 33 year old daughter, Mrs Monica Lilly Charrington. It is not clear how long Sir George had known Mrs Charrington, but they had cruised together to the island of Madeira aboard *Rhouma* in February 1901, where George Bullough had celebrated his thirty-first birthday. Whether it was this particular liaison that resulted in Monica's husband, Charles Edward Nicholas Charrington, petitioning Sir George as co-respondent in his divorce proceedings we can only speculate. The decree was made final and absolute on 25 May 1903. A month later on 24 June, Gerard Gustavus Ducarel, Fourth Marquis de la Pasture, gave his eldest daughter, Monique Lilly,[7] in matrimony to Sir George Bullough in a glittering ceremony at *Kinloch Castle*. A new and even more golden period was about to begin.

Lady Bullough and her entourage heralded a real blossoming at Kinloch. She commandeered the best rooms, the dark air of a gentleman's club was eliminated by the light and elegant hand of a French aristocrat's daughter sweeping over the castle (Figure 14). In 1906, two more floors were built above the west wing to accommodate extra guests and Lady Bullough's personal staff. Greenhouses and palmhouses were supplied by R. Halliday & Co, Middleton, Manchester; Italian gardens and meandering riverside walkways were laid out. French chefs ruled the kitchens, the cellars were stocked with champagne and the very best Madeira wines (Figure 15). The island's population of employees and their families numbered over one hundred, which was considerably increased when the Bulloughs were in residence with their guests and additional staff. Most visits took place for ten or twelve weeks in the autumn, with an occasional one at Christmas and new year (Figure 16). In addition to *Kinloch Castle*, they had a home in London and at *Bishopswood House*, Ross-on-Wye where, on 5 November 1906, Sir George and Lady Bullough's only child, Hermione, was baptised.

The First World War brought ups and downs for Howard and Bullough Ltd and *Kinloch Castle*. Production of munitions between 1914-18 kept Globe Works very busy. The same period heralded the retirement of *Kinloch*, which was on a care and maintenance basis during hostilities, with all the men of fighting age at the front. Of the fourteen gardeners who went to war only two returned. The world had changed; 'being in service' was a thing of the past. The Bulloughs and guests resumed their visits after the war, but it was never to be the same again. The luxury yachts were sold by 1919. There was by now a regular once a week ferry service to Rum, although more geared to carrying livestock than humans and still subject to the vagaries of the weather.

The principal residence was now the *Down House*, Redmarley, Worcester, where Sir George Bullough, Bt (he was raised to the baronetcy in 1916) was Master of the Ledbury Hunt between 1908 and 1922. A major step up the social ladder came with the move to *Warren Hill House*, Newmarket, a magnificent property designed for them in 1928 and where they kept a string of highly successful racehorses. In March 1931 at St Mark's Church, London, Hermione Bullough married Lord Lambton, 5th Earl of Durham. In June 1932 they had a son, the Honourable John George Lambton, who celebrated his twenty-first birthday at *Kinloch Castle* and resides today in London. Hermione, Countess of Durham, died in 1992.

Recession hit the cotton industry in the late 1920s resulting, in

Figure 17. Mausoleum at Harris. John, Sir George and Lady Bullough are all interred here, choosing Rum, the island they loved so much, as their final resting place. *Author's collection*

1933, with the formation of a new merged company, Textile Machinery Makers Ltd, with Sir George as president. The main stakeholders were Howard and Bullough Ltd, with a 25 per cent interest, and Platt Brothers of Oldham with 46 per cent. Inflation, fewer sales, reduced profit and much lower shareholder dividends all combined to put financial pressure on Sir George. His income was greatly reduced. With major costs looming at *Kinloch Castle,* he tried to let and even considered selling the island. His Newmarket home took precedence and the once dream castle was almost abandoned, although it remained staffed. It was, however, starved of its annual 'injection' of the Bulloughs and their guests and the money necessary to maintain everything to the very highest standards for their visits.

Sir George died, aged 69, on 26 July 1939 while playing golf in France. His estate was valued at £714,639 gross, equivalent to about £15 million today. Howard and Bullough Ltd switched to full time war production during the Second World War, increasing the workforce to 6,000. After hostilities ceased, the industrial decline continued. In 1970, the name Platt International replaced that of Howard and Bullough at Globe Works, which still employed 2,200. Further change came in 1975 when Platt, Saco, Lowell became the owner, heralding more redundancies. Platts crashed in 1982, but the works carried on for another eleven years thanks to an American textile magnate. Finally, in 1993, more than a century after it was first built, Globe Works lay idle.

Lady Bullough lived at Newmarket until her death, aged 98, in 1967. Her last visit to *Kinloch Castle* was in 1954 when she drove herself over to Harris to visit the family mausoleum (Figure 17). On 28 February 1957, which would have been Sir George's eighty seventh birthday, Lady Monica Lilly Bullough signed the Minute of Sale transferring the Island of Rum and *Kinloch Castle* to the then Nature Conservancy Council for £23,000. It was the end of a remarkable and never to be repeated era in Britain's industrial and social history.

Kinloch Castle survives! - a credit to the architects who designed it, the men who laboured for three years to build it, the staff who maintained and cleaned it and Sir George Bullough, who had the resources to create and indulge his passion. There resides within most of us a feeling that our home is our castle; if that home happens to be on our own island, so much the better. This 100 year old monument is ours in trust for future generations, an integral part of this country's architectural heritage. The interior is still original and *Kinloch Castle* remains completely furnished awaiting the Bulloughs' return. It is open to the public and guests may stay in hostel-style accommodation.

The *Orchestrion* whirls into action for the entertainment of visitors and, for a few brief moments, if you close your eyes, you are transported back to those carefree days when Edward VII was on the throne, a time before the whole world changed forever with the outbreak of the First World War.

In 1996, Kinloch Castle Friends Association was formed to promote awareness, interest and support for Sir George and Lady Bullough's legacy. 'The Friends' currently has almost 100 members. A newsletter is produced quarterly and regular visits are made to enjoy the island's magnificent scenery and undertake agreed research and restoration tasks associated with the castle. During Association visits, members enjoy several benefits, including the opportunity to have dinner in the Bulloughs' dining room watched over by their portraits. This is living history; there is no better way of experiencing the life and times of Britain's Edwardian era than to visit *Kinloch Castle*.

If you are interested in joining Kinloch Castle Friends Association, contact the secretary and author of this article: George W. Randall, Dentdale, Sedbergh, Cumbria LA10 5RN.

Notes and References

1. John Bullough's letters and speeches were published in three volumes by his wife after his death.
2. R.S. Crossley left a permanent reminder of many important men of Accrington in his *Accrington: Chronological Notes and Men of Mark* and *Accrington Captains of Industry.*
3. Tom Bullough also had a great love for Scotland and bought the Fasnacloich Estate near Ballachulish. He and his wife were considerable benefactors in that area, donating the money for a hospital to be built at Appin. There are several Bullough graves in Appin churchyard.
4. Tweedale and Smalley went on to set up a company together, which was later absorbed into Textile Machinery Makers Ltd. They were both visitors to *Kinloch Castle*, their names appearing in the *Rum Forest Game Books.*
5. The mausoleum and immediate area remain the property of the Bullough Trustees.
6. The leather bound albums are kept in the library at *Kinloch Castle.* Whilst they appear to record a pleasure cruise, careful study has also shown that they indicate an itinerary of actual or potential markets for textile machinery. They also illustrate George Bullough's interest in botany. The plates are of very high quality and are an invaluable record of the world a century ago.
7. French born Monique appears to have used the variation 'Monica' whilst with English people, and the original 'Monique' with her French family.

Acknowledgements

Very special thanks to: Accrington Library Local Studies Department; Mrs Catherine Duckworth, Accrington Library; Mrs June Huntingdon, Accrington; Mr John Kelly, Accrington; Stephen Frankland.

Sources

Subscribers' Report from the Portland Hospital Committee, 1901
Crossley, R.S. *Accrington: Chronological Notes and Men of Mark,* 1924
Crossley, R.S. *Accrington Captains of Industry,* 1930
Rothwell, Mike *Industrial Heritage of Accrington,* 1979
Magnusson, Magnus *Rum: Nature's Island,* 1997
Randall, George W. *Kinloch Castle*
Bullough, John *Speeches and Letters,* 1892

4. POSTED IN ACCRINGTON

by M.D. Booth

ACCRINGTON'S ELEGANT VICTORIAN ARCADE, like many listed buildings, is a fine achievement in design and construction. Yet it is more than an elegant thoroughfare from a bygone age. Riley's Arcade, as it was once known, was one of the first shopping arcades in the country, a forerunner of the impressive shopping malls of today, and for a time was also the centre of post office operations in Accrington (Figure 1). Added to the uniqueness of the Arcade is the fact that it was also the result of private enterprise and the work of one man, Edmund Riley, a fishmonger born in Plantation Square, Accrington (Figure 2).

As a late nineteenth century public building, the Arcade Post Office, clearly at the heart of the community, also provides an insight into the development of the Crown Post Office at the turn of the century and the growing importance of fast, reliable communications. The plans for the Arcade produced for Edmund Riley were designed to accommodate the increasing range of

Figure 1. Postcard of Post Office Arcade, Accrington. The Post Office occupied premises which are now shops on Church Street and was located behind the properties shown here in the Arcade on the left of the picture. See also Figure 9. *Author's Collection.*

Figure 2. Plantation Square, Plantation Street, Accrington 1943. *Lancashire County Council: Accrington Local Studies Library.*

activities of the post office at that time. Significantly, when Edmund Riley built the Arcade in Accrington it was also the first step in the pedestrianisation of the town centre outside the Market Hall. Riley's Arcade, or the Post Office Arcade as it came to be known, was of an age when walking was an enjoyed social experience and even turned into a leisure activity known as promenading. Such habits led to the popularity of the seaside towns and the many Victorian and Edwardian parks in our towns and cities. By bringing the Crown Post Office to the Arcade, Edmund Riley was continuing an improved pattern of movement in the town separating the pedestrian from the increasing number of vehicles in Accrington's town centre. The Arcade provided citizens with a sheltered and well-illuminated walk; its gentle curved plan also added further interest. In design, the Arcade clearly belonged to that great Victorian and Edwardian era of the railway station, theatre, promenade and the pier.

Yet the construction of the Arcade was also a far-sighted experiment in town planning. Sadly, it has taken a century of experience of the motor vehicle to realise that town planners would have achieved far more if they had recognised earlier that towns and cities are primarily for people and not vehicles. The twentieth century has been dominated by the onslaught of the internal combustion engine and town planners have been compelled to attend to the demand for more and more roads. Now draconian legislation seems to be needed to establish an integrated transport system to combat the increasing gridlock and pollution problems in our cities.

Fortunately, Accrington's town centre has retained most of its civic identity. Its people still have the freedom to walk for a large part without the excesses of motor traffic and the authorities have established some equilibrium with parking. With so many larger towns forced apart by traffic routes which have destroyed any semblance of a distinct municipal character, Accrington has indeed been fortunate in avoiding some of the worst ravages. At the end of the twentieth century, the Arcade is a useful reminder of what town life was beginning to achieve and is now turning towards once more.

Figure 3. Edmund Riley.
Lancashire County Council:
Accrington Local Studies Library.

When Edmund Riley (Figure 3), one time Market Hall fishmonger and local councillor, in that late Victorian celebration of civic pride, industry and Empire, decided to build the Arcade, he also succeeded in capturing that nineteenth century confidence and boldness in British industry and commerce. It is this spirit of enterprise, pride and optimism embodied in the Arcade that we should recognise when we walk through this thoroughfare today and not the empty shops or signs of decay.

The Post Office Arcade centred the town more clearly in the Church Street area. Yet the short life of the Crown Post Office in the Arcade was the result of the same communication revolution which began the twentieth century and now appears to be bringing in its close with new changes based on computer technology and the Internet. A century of telecommunications has resulted in the amazing development of powers in the circulation of information globally. The process started early. In the 1900s, the Post Office Arcade soon proved unsuitable because of the increasing use of the telephone for communication. Yet the facilities in the Arcade were

Figure 4. Abbey Street Post Office, No 30 to the right of Jonathan Welch, the tailor at No 32; both these premises are now occupied by a firm of soft furnishing specialists. *Lancashire County Council: Accrington Local Studies Library*

once purpose built and assisted a prosperous and growing community to communicate more effectively with the rest of the world. How rapidly this revolution has come about.

For most of the nineteenth century, the organisation of the mail was extremely primitive. Earlier post offices had existed on Abbey Street and Bridge Street in the centre of Accrington, but they had never enjoyed sufficient accommodation or prominence. The Royal Mail had relied on the stagecoach which journeyed via Abbey Street until 1848. When the railway arrived the same year, it seems Accrington had no sorting office for local mail and this had to be carried out at Preston. At one time the postmaster of the earliest Post Office in Abbey Street, Robert Holt, also used the premises as a barber's shop (Figure 4).

Later in the 1850s, the town's post office was housed in the Peel Institution, now the Town Hall. The rent of £20 per annum seemed excessive to the postmaster, William Ponsonby Weddall, owing to the fact that he only received an annual salary of £45 and he was often

Figure 5. Blackburn Road, Accrington in the 1890s from the Town Hall, or Peel Institution, showing the junction with Church Street to the right in the middle ground. The shop on the extreme right of the picture is on the corner of Dutton Street. The amount of activity on this busy thoroughfare emphasises the need for pedestrianised shopping facilities. *Lancashire County Council: Accrington Local Studies Library*

in attendance for up to seventeen hours a day in a badly ventilated room. Fortunately for him, postmaster Weddall managed to persuade the authorities that he would be able to carry out his duties more easily in premises at 11 Dutton Street which were adjacent to his home residence (Figure 5). A petition, taken at the counter, supported the request and eventually the authorities were convinced that the Weddall family (they were described as a strange couple) could perform the duties required of a postmaster in 1860 from this cottage in Dutton Street. Centrally located this is where Accrington's main post office operated until 1880. As well as postmaster for Accrington, he was also the distributor of Inland Revenue Stamps and collected the death duty. There were no parcel post, postal orders or telephones and only the most important messages were relayed over the telegraph wires. The telegraph was not a welcome delivery; to most minds the telegraph messenger in those days was usually associated with the announcement of a death in the family.

The Post Office remained at the Dutton Street location for nearly twenty years until it moved to Church Street. The former location next to their own home suited the Weddall family and it is easy to see why. When the mail cart arrived from Burnley at 10.00pm on its journey to Preston via Blackburn, this marked the end of a long day which started at 4.20am each morning. William Weddall and his family witnessed the growth in mail from 5,000 to 26,000 letters a week during his 32 years as Accrington's postmaster. Later their son, John Weddall, also served in the postal service as a sub-postmaster on Blackburn Road. The family must have been well trained in the operations of the Post Office.

The Weddall family operated a Crown Post Office from larger premises on Church Street from 1880 onwards, but it appears that no purpose built sorting office in Accrington existed for a considerable part of the nineteenth century. It is typical of the period that the Accrington Crown Post Office at that time relied completely on male operatives, with no facilities for women clerks or telegraphists on the premises.

In 1894, Edmund Riley took on the task of keeping the Crown Post Office in the centre of Accrington and a large sorting office was included in the plan for the Arcade. When the architects, Haywood and Harrison, drew up the plans for Edmund Riley, the work involved the demolition of the existing Post Office which fronted onto Church Street. By the early 1890s, the activities required the use of six rooms in the building on Church Street (Figure 6). The postmaster general, keen to

Figure 6. Old Post Office, Church Street, Accrington. *Lancashire County Council: Accrington Local Studies Library*

Figure 7. Church Street before construction of the Arcade pre 1894.
Accrington Observer.

minimise any unnecessary further expenditure, accepted Edmund
Riley's offer to re-house the Post Office inside the Arcade at a rent of
£230 on a 21 year lease. Interestingly, one of the considerations in
the calculations identified a saving of £73 by means of the
substitution of 4 women for 4 male sorting clerks and telegraphists.

The row of elegant Victorian shops on this section of Church
Street, still in existence today, was also the property of Edmund
Riley; his game and fishmonger's shop was situated at the Blackburn
Road end of the row (Figure 7).

Although a member of Accrington's first town council of 1879,
representing the north east ward, Edmund Riley of 135 Burnley
Road Accrington seemed often at odds with them. He preferred to
concentrate his efforts on ambitious business projects connected
with the development of the Church Street complex to create that
wonderful Victorian mixture of shopping and entertainment. Sadly,
his dreams of creating a theatre in the Arcade and an ice rink on Peel

NEW POST OFFICE AND ARCADE AT ACCRINGTON.

Figure 8. New Post Office and Arcade, Accrington. *Accrington Observer and Times,* 29 September, 1894

Figure 9. Ground plan of Post Office Arcade, Accrington. *Accrington Observer and Times,* 29 September 1894

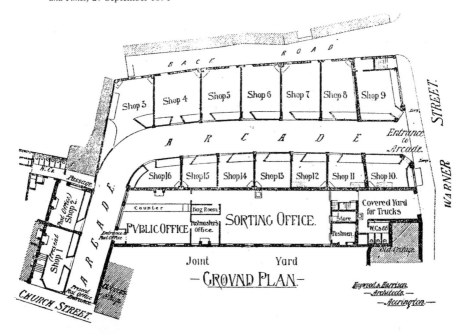

Street failed dramatically and he eventually lost £700 on the latter, but his boldness can still be admired.

When the new Post Office was opened to the public on Monday 12 October 1894, it was a showpiece of local craftsmanship and Accrington brick. The intricate patterns of the leaded lights above the shop windows denote clearly that the Arcade was one man's extravagant dream using all the ingenuity available at the end of the nineteenth century (Figure 8). The extent of the late nineteenth century Post Office building is not fully appreciated until the ground plan is examined and the three storey building on Warner Street is included (Figure 9). The internal fittings provided by the Post Office in the public areas were also impressive. Characteristically, the 35 feet long polished teak counter was fronted with a brass guard 'in order that the public property may be protected'. Even at the opening of the building the reporter recorded that 'it (the sorting office) has not been made sufficiently large, and it is expected that in a very short time owing to the rapid growth of the town it will be too small.' Indeed, the rapid expansion of the telephone service by 1910 ensured that the Post Office was set to leave Riley's Arcade by 1917 on the expiry of the 21 year lease. Such plans were overtaken by the outbreak of war in 1914.

Inevitably, the war placed far greater demands on the Post Office than ever before, a time when more mail and parcels left Accrington for foreign fields. The Great War, 1914-1918, delayed the eventual relocation to its present site until October 1922. The old sorting office somehow coped. The telegraph system kept up with the increased demands and the telephone exchange developed accordingly.

Today, the relatively brief existence of the Crown Post Office in the Arcade is marked only by the two words, POST OFFICE, high up above the old entrance, yet what communications it dealt with during those momentous years! Hopefully, the vision that created the Post Office Arcade at the end of the nineteenth century will be appreciated in the twenty-first century. Could such a place lend itself to a technology revolution once again?

Acknowledgements

I acknowledge with grateful thanks Lancashire County Council: Accrington Local Studies Library for kind permission to reproduce Figures 2-6.

5. Canal Workers and Boatmen Around Accrington

by Mike Clarke

THE LEEDS & LIVERPOOL CANAL was not originally intended to serve the towns of East Lancashire. It was planned to follow a route to the north of the River Calder, crossing into the Ribble Valley over an aqueduct at Whalley Nab. Limestone was considered to be the canal's most significant traffic and this route would have enabled the quarries at Clitheroe to be served by a branch. The canal took many years to build and, by the time it had climbed out of the Aire Valley at Gargrave, it was realised that the growing East Lancashire industries would provide much traffic. The route was altered so that the canal passed through Burnley, which it reached in 1796 (Figure 1). It was extended to Enfield Wharf in 1801, some 31 years after construction of the canal had begun. A further nine years were to pass before it opened to Blackburn, since there were difficulties in

Figure 1. A 1792 map of the canal showing the original line which would have passed nearer to Accrington. The actual line passed to the other side of the community at Church, rejoining the original line by a right angle bend between points L and K. *Author's collection*

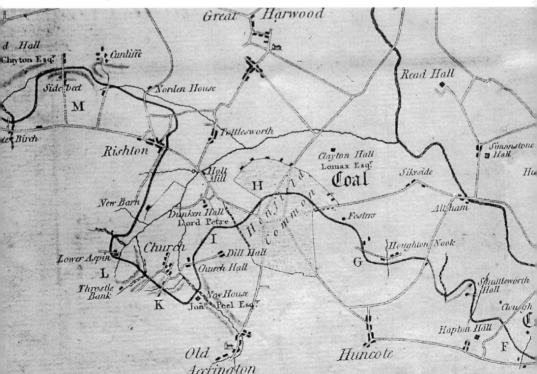

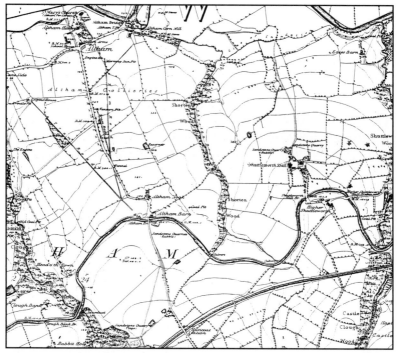

Figure 2. Extract from the 1848 Ordnance Survey (1:10560) first edition map of Altham showing tram roads from collieries to the canal. *Lancashire County Council: Accrington Local Studies Library*

crossing the many rivers and streams around Church and the deep cutting at Sidebeet also took time to complete. The through route by water between Liverpool and Leeds was eventually completed in 1816.

It may have taken a long time to build, but the canal soon became an important factor in the growth of industry in East Lancashire. The cheap and reliable transport it provided allowed not only general goods but also bulk cargoes to be carried easily. Raw materials for the rapidly expanding textile trades came from both Liverpool and Hull, whilst stone flags, limestone and coal were carried to and from wharves all along the canal. The shallow coalfield around Altham expanded after the canal opened, allowing the coal to reach new markets and tramroads were built between the pits in the Calder Valley and the canal at Altham Barn Bridge (Figure 2). Today it is hard to imagine that for half of the nineteenth century this was a bustling industrial community.

During this period, a packet boat, carrying passengers and small packets up to 56lbs in weight, operated daily between Burnley and Blackburn. It called at several places along the way, including Altham Barn Bridge, where it served local miners, agricultural and other workers. Amongst them were several boatmen and their families whose boats delivered coal from Altham to wharves along the canal in East Lancashire. With a cargo of 40 tons or more, the barges carried enough to ensure that the boatmen and their families had a good standard of living. They usually lived in a house and, although one son often helped his father on the boat, any other children usually worked in local industries.

Boatmen and their families around Altham

On the Leeds & Liverpool Canal there were two distinctive ways of working a boat. There were the long-distance boatmen who lived aboard and travelled the whole length of the canal, carrying general cargoes such as machinery, groceries and other package goods, and there were those who carried coal and bulk cargoes who travelled shorter distances and were often able to return home at night. Both

Figure 3. Conditions for boatmen were not idyllic. The motor and dumb coal boats here are returning empty to Bank Hall Colliery, Burnley, after unloading at Whitebirk Power Station, circa 1955. The black diamond motif was used by Crooke & Thompson and their successors, Messrs Hargreaves. Note the open hold, lack of coamings and shovels for unloading, typical of Leeds & Liverpool Canal coal boats. *Author's collection*

earned enough to have a house as well as a boat, with many long-distance boatmen coming from the Burscough area. Coal boatmen tended to live in houses close to the supply of coal, moving when the colliery closed. In the middle of the nineteenth century, there was a small community of boatmen at Altham who worked the boats carrying coal from the small collieries in the Calder Valley (Figure 3).

A number of boatmen are listed in the census as living around Altham. In 1841, at Houghton Nook, lived the Pilkingtons, Benjamin, Henry, Robert and John, as well as John Waddington, whilst John Hoyle lived at Clough Bank. Their ages ranged from fourteen to thirty. By 1851, there were eight boatmen listed in Altham, all of them born locally. It would seem that, with the growth of the coal industry and the associated demand for transport, they had become boatmen to work on the boats carrying coal from Altham. Their ages ranged from seventeen to forty-three and their employment as boatmen certainly seems to be linked to the growth of the coalmines around Altham.

Pilkington was a common name in the area, so it is small surprise that boatmen with this family name appear in the census both at Altham and Enfield. Some attended Altham Church whose parish registers list baptisms and deaths for members of boatmen's families. Others attended Church Kirk where amongst other entries Thomas Haworth, a boatman from Altham, married Elizabeth Newsham from Huncoat in 1847. The same names recur as, once established,

Figure 4. This boat, shown at West End, Oswaldtwistle, was cut down and used by Croasdale's for carrying coal from Bank Hall to Whitebirk. It was formerly one of Appleby's grain boats, from Enfield. *Lancashire County Council: Accrington Local Studies Library*

families maintained their links with work on the canal, moving along its length to follow the best opportunities for work.

By the time of the 1881 census, there was just one boating family listed around Altham, that of John Metcalf. He lived at Rosy Bank (just by the Vitriol Works!), with his wife, three daughters and five sons, one of whom, also called John, worked on the canal. By 1891, there were no boatmen or their families listed in Altham's census. By this time the small coalmines in the Calder Valley had ceased to be viable with mining being concentrated on the deeper pits, such as Huncoat or Moorfield, causing the boatmen and their families to move away.

In the twentieth century, communities of boating families became less common as traffic on the canal slowly declined. In East Lancashire, a few lived close together at Mill Hill in Blackburn, but most lived as part of the wider working community, although usually not too far from the canal. Boatmen from this area worked on coal boats on the canal between Burnley and Wigan. As the railway ran parallel to the canal for much of this length, it was easy for them to get home at night and back to the boat in the morning. As long distance traffic declined, a number of boatmen from these boats also settled locally to work on the boats carrying coal from Bank Hall Colliery to the power station at Whitebirk (Figure 4).

The warehouses at Enfield and Church

General cargoes carried by canal to and from the Accrington district were handled at warehouses at Enfield and Church. The canal's terminus from 1801 to 1810 was Enfield, the warehouse here being convenient for the turnpikes to Blackburn, Bury and Clitheroe. It was not only local goods which were handled at this time, but also those travelling from Hull and the textile areas of the West Riding to Liverpool and Manchester. Until the canal was completed to Blackburn, goods had to be transshipped here for onward delivery. At first, all traffic to and from the area used Enfield warehouse. It was developed over the years, with extensions and new buildings being added on several occasions on both sides of the canal.

One of the earliest agents for the canal company at Enfield was John Walls who worked there around 1830. The canal company only began its own carrying fleet in 1848 and, earlier, there were private fleets of boats on the canal. These fleets carried general cargoes, whilst bulk cargoes such as coal were always carried by privately owned boats. At Enfield in 1834, Richard Eatough represented Tyrer, Rigby & Co, and Jno Bickersteth the Leeds Union, two of the

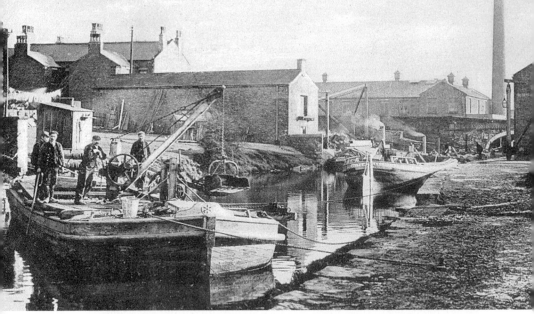

Figure 5. A view of Enfield Wharf around the time of the First World War. The boat in the foreground is a spoon dredger, the spoon being filled with mud by manipulation by hand and then raised using the crane. In the background, boats are waiting after unloading, possibly for the regular steam tug employed on this length of canal. The main warehouse is on the left, the wharf and crane in the centre of the picture being used mainly for timber. The factory beyond the bridge is the old Taywil works. *Author's collection*

most important general cargo carriers on the canal in the first half of the nineteenth century. There were several houses at Enfield Wharf and a later canal agent, William Harrison, lived at no 99 with his wife, two sons and a daughter in 1851. William came from Skipton and presumably had previously worked on the canal there. One son helped at the wharf, as did Richard Eatough who lived with his family at no 100, whilst Nancy Pilkington, the owner of a local farm, lived at no 101 with her two boatmen sons. Three years later, Richard Eatough had become canal agent and was aided by his clerk, John Walls. Perhaps this is the John Walls who had been canal agent in the 1830s. Eatough was still at Enfield in 1861 but, by 1871, had been replaced by Edward Jackson who came from Clayton-le-Dale, another place served by the canal. In turn, John Turner from Burnley had replaced him by 1881 and Frank George then took over around 1885.

Due to railway competition, the canal company stopped carrying general cargo on their own boats around 1850 and a group of railway companies took out a lease for this traffic. They continued to carry general cargoes, but worked at diverting traffic to their own railway lines. By 1870, the Lancashire & Yorkshire Railway had a virtual monopoly of general goods traffic in East Lancashire, but were providing a poor service. Local mill owners and merchants complained to the canal company, asking them to take back the lease and start carrying general cargoes once more. So, in 1874, the Leeds & Liverpool Canal Company re-formed their fleet of barges, improving facilities at warehouses and were soon taking back much traffic from the railways. They did this to such an extent that the Lancashire & Yorkshire Railway Company were having to lay off staff at Burnley in 1880.

William Henry Pugh was in charge of Enfield Wharf from about 1888. He came with his family from Shropshire, one of many immigrants to East Lancashire at that time. Not only did the textile industry require more labour, but the canal had also been revitalised in the 1870s and 1880s and a number of people came from canals in the Midlands to work on the Leeds & Liverpool. William Pugh stayed until just before the First World War when he was promoted to be agent at Foulridge and William Taberner took over at Enfield from around 1912 until 1921. He was paid £80 per annum and allowed to live in the wharf house without charge (Figure 5).

Unfortunately, the First World War seriously affected the profitability of the canal when it was placed under government control. To improve their finances, the canal company sold their fleet in 1921 and, in East Lancashire, they were taken over by Lancashire

Figure 6. Church Wharf just after 1900, with two Leeds & Liverpool Canal Company boats unloading cotton. They are dumb boats which would probably have been towed by a steam barge from Liverpool. The boatmen lived in a cabin under the stern deck. Note the water barrels and the ventilator box on boat 220. The decoration on the boats is typical of that used on the Leeds & Liverpool canal where scrolls and geometric patterns were used extensively. *Lancashire County Council: Accrington Local Studies Library*

Canal Transport. William Hammond became their agent at Enfield, staying there when a new firm, Canal Transport Limited, was formed in 1930 to carry all general cargoes on the canal. He seems to have retired during the Second World War and most trade was then handled at the wharves at Church.

It is uncertain when the first wharf at Church was established. As originally planned, the canal would have continued up the valley of the Hyndburn into Accrington but, in order to avoid the Peel Bank Printworks, the route was altered. Instead it passed on the lower side of the print works leaving Accrington about a mile from the canal. Consequently, all goods to and from Accrington had to be transshipped at Enfield or Church. The Hargreaves brothers built a warehouse at Church, on the new turnpike road to Blackburn, in 1836 for goods manufactured at their Broad Oak Printworks. A wharf was erected for them seven years later, the canal company draining the canal for just 24 hours to allow the foundations to be built. The canal company may also have operated a wharf here from around 1830, perhaps put in at the same time as the turnpike was built circa 1826. Hargreaves' warehouse was subsequently taken over by the canal company in 1890 to become the main canal warehouse in the area for a period (Figure 6). However, with the growth of Howard and Bullough's trade in exporting textile machinery, a new wharf was opened near Bradley Street sometime in the 1890s, where the machinery could be stored before onward delivery. Both wharves at Church were used simultaneously for a period, but by the 1930s all trade had been concentrated at Bradley Street. Several new warehouses were erected here over the years and it was not until around 1960 that the last warehouse was built here by the canal company.

Three carrying firms are certainly recorded as serving the area in 1848. One, Tyrer and Glovers, had one of the largest fleets serving places all along the canal. The other two, the Chaffer brothers and Isabella Crabtree, were more concerned with traffic to East Lancashire, Isabella also running the packet boat between Blackburn and Burnley. Originally, cargo handling at Church and Enfield may have come under the control of one agent, but the wharf next to the warehouse, behind the Commercial Hotel, seems to have been operated separately from around 1881 when a canal agent, Isaac Smith, was listed in local directories as being based at Church. He was succeeded by John W. Varley in 1891, who was subsequently dismissed because of irregularities in his accounts. He was assisted in his work around the wharf by W. Prince and J.H. Banner who both left together in 1895. Turnover of staff was quite frequent, with the clerk here earning £50 per annum in 1908 compared with £140 per annum for the agent.

There was a serious accident at the wharf in August 1899 when William Worsick, a labourer living at 16 Walker Street, Church, was killed by the crane on the corner of the warehouse. He was working with the hand-powered crane, engaged in hoisting packs of flour into the boat. He was putting the crane out of its 'little' gear into the 'big' gear as was normal when lowering a cargo. Unfortunately, the handle slipped, striking him in the breast and knocking him backwards into a boat. Dr Craig who attended him ordered him to be taken to Accrington Cottage Hospital where he died on the following Sunday. At the inquest it was stated that the crane was lifting three packs of flour at the time. The verdict was 'Accidental Death'. Flour and grain were important cargoes on the canal, the tonnage carried at the end of the nineteenth century being equal to the tonnage of cotton carried.

Herbert Grant had become agent by 1903 but was replaced by John Abraham by 1912. The First World War brought further changes; Ben Taylor was in charge in 1915, followed by Harry Schofield in 1918. By this time the agent's office had moved to the wharf at the back of Bradley Street which the agent now ran in conjunction with the warehouse on Blackburn Road.

The wharf near Bradley Street was used principally for Howard and Bullough's export trade. Cases of textile machinery were stored here until the ship in which they were to be exported had almost finished loading. Word was sent from Liverpool for the cases of machinery to be loaded into canal boats, which delivered them straight to the ship's side. Machinery in cases was a light cargo, easily damaged if stored in the docks and it, therefore, had to be loaded on top of other cargo. The journey time from Church to Liverpool by canal was around eighteen hours travelling non-stop. Most general cargoes on the canal came from Liverpool to East Lancashire, so this return traffic was very important to the canal company to prevent boats returning empty to Liverpool. They certainly cultivated Howard and Bulloughs who were the first customers to be invited out for a day on the canal company's inspection boat *Waterwitch*.

Large stables were provided at the Bradley Street wharf. The horses using them were not only boat horses, but also those used for local deliveries, such as collecting the cases of machinery from Howard and Bullough. At the turn of the century, Thomas Crawshaw, a local coal merchant, provided the collection and

Figures 7 and 8. Two views of one of the modern warehouses at Church. The overhead gantry was used for loading boats. Behind the warehouse, the stables damaged in the Canary Isle explosion during the First World War can be seen. The interior view shows crates of machinery from Howard and Bulloughs and other items from GEC awaiting onward delivery. *Author's collection*

delivery service from the wharf. He was obviously not too reliable as the canal company took over this part of his business in 1901, paying £700 for his stable, horses and lurries, less than half Crawshaw's asking price. In 1907, a new lurry for Church was ordered from Henry Eaton of Manchester at a cost of £35 12s 6d, slightly less than the cost of a horse. Facilities for handling cargoes improved in 1913 when an electric crane was installed to help with loading and unloading.

During the First World War, there was an explosion at the chemical works opposite the Bradley Street canal wharf. Four boats and a steam tug were passing at the time and the sheets covering their cargoes damaged. The canal company's report stated that the electric travelling and steam derrick cranes were slightly damaged; cases of machinery belonging to Howard and Bullough, protected by waterproof covers, were set on fire; and the electric switch house and stabling consisting of nineteen stalls with lofts over them, three loose boxes, cart shed and harness room were more or less demolished. The horses were rescued uninjured. Owing to war conditions only nine horses had been employed at the wharf, whereas in normal times the stabling would have been fully occupied.

During the war, the canal was run by a government committee and soldiers were employed on some of the boats, a battalion of the South Lancashire Regiment being established for this purpose. Maintenance was a low priority and, when the canal was handed back to the canal company, insufficient compensation was paid for the deterioration in its condition. As stated above, the canal company gave up carrying in 1921 and the service was continued by Lancashire Canal Transport. At Church in 1924, their agent was James Draper, a surname fairly common amongst those working on boats on the canal.

Church became the main centre for cargoes to and from the Accrington district following the formation of Canal Transport Limited in 1930, when Lancashire Canal Transport amalgamated with three other firms to form the new company. It was around this time that the Blackburn Road warehouse ceased to be used for canal cargoes, with all goods then handled from the Bradley Street wharf where Howard and Bullough continued to be important customers. Facilities for this traffic were improved regularly with the construction of several new warehouses, the last one in the 1950s. This had an overhead crane which stretched out right across the canal, making loading and unloading of boats very easy (Figures 7 and 8).

The canal had been nationalised by this time and the Church wharf formed part of the Blackburn Depot. Nine men were employed at Church under Depot Superintendent Jack Hunter. Others included the warehouse clerk, A.B. Parsons, crane drivers J. Archer and W.R. Fielding and porter J.W. Margerison. Carrying by boat finished around 1963, but Church Depot continued to be used for storage of goods carried by road vehicles until 1985, when a fire destroyed the largest warehouse.

The Boats and Boatmen

The families of canal boatmen are always difficult to trace from the census as they could be on board their boat when it was being taken. Boats were not included on the census until 1861 when a special form for boats was provided but was not always used; perhaps they were difficult to obtain so far inland. Even with these forms, as boats sometimes travelled by night, the boatmen were often ignored by the census takers, who probably did not consider them resident in the area at the time of the census. There was, at one time in the late-nineteenth century, over 1000 boats working on the Leeds & Liverpool Canal. As there were at least two boatmen per boat, this means that at least twice that number of boatmen must have been employed. However, nothing like this number appears in the census, with just the occasional boat being mentioned.

Although the only additional information recorded by the census was the boat's name, with tonnage, cargo and owner sometimes included if the correct form were used, it is possible to create quite a detailed picture of the people and the boat in question. For example, the 1871 census includes two boats which were tied up at Enfield. The first boat was the *Mendel,* carrying 40 tons of goods with its captain Robert Varley, who had been born in Skipton. He was 40 years old and, as Varley is an unusual name on the canal, his son may have been the John W. Varley who had to leave Church warehouse in disgrace in the 1890s. Mate on the boat was William Walker from Liverpool. With just two men on board, each coming from a town away from East Lancashire, this suggests that the *Mendel* was a horse-drawn general cargo boat carrying goods along the whole length of the canal.

The other boat tied up at Enfield on that night was the *Swan of Burnley,* with captain Elijah Duckworth from Marsden and mate Thomas Hirst from Briercliffe. The boat is recorded as carrying 40 tons of coal, a cargo which any boat coming from Burnley, with a crew also born in the area, would almost certainly have been carrying. Coal boats from Burnley did not travel great distances, usually restricted to the canal between Skipton and Blackburn. Other sections of the canal had their own coal supplies. The Wigan coalfield supplied the length from Liverpool to Blackburn, whilst West Yorkshire coal was carried up the Aire Valley to Skipton and occasionally as far as Barnoldswick. In the nineteenth century, coal boats often had their home town added to their name.

Figure 9. Four men are using shovels and barrows to unload the coal barge the *Margaret* on the canal by Bolton Road, opposite Blackburn Royal Infirmary. Photograph taken by E. Carr of Clayton-le-Moors and donated to Accrington Library by Fred Rogers. *Lancashire County Council: Accrington Local Studies Library*

In the 1881 census, there was only one boat tied up at Enfield, the *Anne*. Captain William Watkinson was accompanied by his wife Elizabeth and three children, James (four), Alice (two) and Robert (nine months), as well as the mate James Watkinson, probably his brother. They had all been born in Burscough or Lathom, which was an area where most of the long-distance Leeds & Liverpool boatmen originated. Even today, it is possible to wander around Burscough and its outskirts and see houses built specifically for boatmen with the stable for the boathorse built at the back. As the crew came from Burscough, the boat was probably carrying general cargo or grain. With a family on board it was more likely to be the latter, since general cargo boats were somewhat more controlled in their operation. In the nineteenth century, it was not too unusual for families to live on board. It was the introduction of the steam engine and later the diesel engine, which led to the virtual elimination of this facet of canal life. However, there were several married couples who worked their own boat in the twentieth century, although their children would only accompany them during the school holidays.

Also in 1881, there were four boats tied up at Church, the crews mainly coming from the Burscough area. As general cargo boats would usually have been tied up here, this was to be expected. There was one boat with Joseph Taylor from Newburgh (near Burscough) as captain with three crew members. Normally this would suggest that the boat was a flyboat. These worked non-stop, often towed by a steam tug in Lancashire, with one or two of the crew sleeping on the lengths between the flights of locks. However, the others in the crew were Joseph (22), Samuel (20) and Margaret Taylor (18), all born in Runcorn. Joseph is described as mate, whilst Samuel is listed as steward. Perhaps this was a family group, with the three from Runcorn taking the chance for a holiday on their uncle's boat. Samuel is certainly the only steward I have found in the census working on a canal boat! Family members having a holiday on board was not unusual on the canal, whilst there are also recorded instances of European emigrants making their way from Hull to Liverpool by canal to catch a boat to America.

The 1891 census provides details of two more boats tied up at Church. The first was boat *Amy no 178*; the number was either the boat's canal company number since names were changed to numbers in the 1890s, or its registered number. From 1878, boats had to be registered with the local authority whose public health staff would check the boat's cabins to ensure they were clean, free from vermin and that there were not too many people living on board. Some of the registration books still survive in record offices. Robert Seddon (48) was the captain of the *Amy*, with a crew of Thomas (18) and Edward (13), all three from Whittle, and James Brawdon (14) from Wigan. This was almost certainly a coal boat carrying coal from Wigan. A crew of two was usually enough for handling the boat, so perhaps the others had come along to help unload the cargo. Using a shovel and barrow, it was a day's work for four men to unload a cargo of 45 tons (Figure 9). Often there were local men who specialised in this job. However, they had to be paid, so this crew were probably trying to keep the money within their own family. Also tied up was *Macbeth*, with Robert Howard (30) captain, and Thomas Eccleston (17) mate, both from Burscough, so this was almost certainly a general cargo boat.

At Rishton in the 1891 census, there was recorded a 'boat on canal'. The crew were waterman Noah Colclough, born Wolverhampton, Mary Colclough, born Stoke Prior, Thomas Colclough, born Runcorn and mate, Joseph Moores from Manchester. Also on board was Joseph Horsfield from Hyde, who was the boat's owner. He was a well-known boat owner, whose fleet of boats was based on the Bridgewater Canal. They continued to trade until the 1960s with the firm's headquarters at Runcorn. By then they were all narrow boats but in the earlier days the fleet certainly included wide boats. This was probably one of them, although he may also have had shortened narrow boats which were capable of working through the 60 feet long Leeds & Liverpool locks. Narrow boats were usually 72 feet in length.

The Colcloughs came from the narrow canals of the Midlands to work on the Leeds & Liverpool Canal, as did several other such families at the end of the nineteenth century. The improvement to cargo carrying services on the canal through the 1880s and 1890s encouraged narrow boatmen to make the change at a time when traffic on some narrow canals was beginning to decline. The Salt family was another family attracted to East Lancashire by better work prospects. They originally worked on the shortened narrow boats which brought salt from Middlewich to the chemical works in Church. When Blythes decided to have their own boats, the Salts were asked to move to Church to become boatmen on the Leeds & Liverpool Canal.

For almost two hundred years, the Leeds & Liverpool Canal has served the people of East Lancashire. Not only did it encourage the development of local industries, but it also created a link to other communities, allowing working people to move between jobs. Today, it still has an impact on our lives, bringing a reminder of less-hurried days and creating a linear park which brings the countryside closer to even the most industrial areas. It is your inheritance; use it for your leisure, but do not forget those for whom it was a living and a way of life.

Acknowledgements

I would like to thank Lancashire County Council: Accrington Local Studies Library for kind permission to reproduce photographs in this article.

6. HENRY WATSON (1846-1911): A MUSICAL LIFE

by June Tomlinson

AVANT-GARDE COMPOSER, SIR HARRISON BIRTWISTLE, and operatic bass, John Tomlinson, of Huncoat and Oswaldtwistle origins respectively, are acclaimed twentieth-century sons of Hyndburn who have achieved international musical stature. Both are alumni of the Royal Northern College of Music, but another talented musician with Accrington roots had also been associated with this institution since its foundation in 1893. Dr Henry Watson made a significant donation to the RNCM of his collection of 300 musical instruments, whilst his library of books and music was gifted to the Corporation of Manchester during his lifetime. The Henry Watson Music Library – its very name perpetuating the memory of its founder – has been housed within the imposing Central Reference Library in St Peter's Square, Manchester since 1947 and has expanded in the space of a century from the original 16,700 volumes in 1899 to some 600,000 volumes today.

Birth

Henry Watson was born on 30 April 1846 at West Gate, in the township of Habergham Eaves, Burnley (Figure 1).[1] His parents were Sarah Watson, formerly Holt, and Thomas Watson, who gave his occupation as 'overlooker in a mill' and signed the register with his mark, a possible indication of illiteracy.[2]

CERTIFICATE SUMMARY SHEET for *Henry WATSON*

	Registration District *Burnley*								
1846 **BIRTH** in the Sub-district of *Burnley* .... in the									
1	2	3	4	5	6	7	8	9	10
No.	When and where born	Name, if any	Sex	Name and surname of father	Name, surname & maiden name of mother	Occupation of father	Signature, description etc of informant	When registered	Signature of registrar	Name after registration
435	30 April 1846 West Gate Habergham Eaves	Henry		Thomas WATSON	Sarah WATSON formerly HOLT	Overlooker in a mill	The mark X of Thomas Watson, father	3 June 1846		
.... Superintendent Registrar .... Date									

Figure 1. Copy of birth certificate of Henry Watson for 1846 held at the Henry Watson Music Library, Manchester Central Library.

Census

According to the *Musical Times*, which interviewed Dr Watson in 1909,

> *at the age of three, Henry lost the most precious treasure that a child can possess - his mother. Soon afterwards his father married again, and the family removed to Accrington.*[3]

The *Accrington Observer and Times* stated in its obituary notice of 1911 that Dr Watson was 'brought to Accrington when a child by his parents, who lived in Wellington Street'.[4] Together, these separate sources suggest that Henry's birth mother died circa 1849-50 and that by the time of the 1851 census the family, augmented by a second Mrs Watson, was living in Accrington, possibly on Wellington Street. However, scrutiny of each occurrence of the name Watson in the Accrington 1851 census schedules did not locate the family in the town; nor were they to be found otherwise by double-checking all the Wellington Street returns.[5]

Moving the census search back a decade to Henry's Westgate birthplace in the Burnley 1841 schedules also failed to uncover any Watsons at that location. Ultimately, however, the surname index to heads of households in the Burnley 1851 schedules, amongst which were listed two instances of 'Thomas Watson, overlooker', led to the relevant entry below (Figure 2):[6]

Figure 2. 1851 Census Return for the Watson Family

Township: Habergham Eaves			**Ecclesiastical district:** The Holy Trinity			
Address	Name	Rel.[1]	Cond.[2]	Age	Occupation	Where born
1 Watkinson's Court	Thomas Watson	Head	M	35	Overlooker in a Cotton Mill	York: Earby
	Sarah Watson	Wife	M	39		Lancaster: Barrowford
	Joseph Watson	Son		13	Piece Hooker Do.Do.	Lancaster: Barrowford
	Henry Watson	Son		4	Scholar	Lancaster: Habergham Eaves
	John Holt	Lodger	U	25	Power Loom Weaver (Cotton)	Lancaster: Trawden

Abbreviations: Rel.[1] Relation to Head of Family
              Cond.[2] Condition, ie whether married

Watkinson's Court, which immediately follows 34 Westgate in the enumerator's schedules, does not appear on the 1848 six-inch Ordnance Survey map of the area, suggesting that it had been recently-built at the time the family lived there. It is noteworthy that Henry Watson's mother Sarah was still alive in 1851 as he approached his fifth birthday, in contradiction to the childhood memory cited in his 1909 interview. The census also reveals that Henry had a brother Joseph, nine years his senior, a fact not disclosed elsewhere in printed sources.

Furthermore, the 1851 census provides a significant clue as to the whereabouts of the Watson family ten years earlier. Thirteen-year old Joseph is recorded in 1851 as being born in Barrowford five miles to the north and, following this lead, a search of the Barrowford 1841 census schedules did locate the family there (Figure 3).

Figure 3. 1841 Census Return for the Watson Family

Address	Name	Age	Occupation	Whether born in same county
Barrowford	Thomas Watson	20	Cotton weaver	N
	Sarah Watson	20		Y
	Joseph Watson	2		Y

Cotton Industry

It was no secret during Dr Watson's lifetime that 'his father was connected, in no imposing office, with the cotton industry of the Burnley district', and we have seen that Thomas Watson's occupation was recorded during the 1841 Barrowford census as being that of a cotton weaver.[7] By the time of Henry's birth in 1846 the family had moved to Burnley and Thomas had progressed to the position of an overlooker in a cotton mill. Although he could not write his name on registering his son's birth, his employment was not without skill or responsibility. The overlooker, or 'tackler', saw to the smooth running of the machinery in the mill; in Aspin's harsh assessment, 'as chief administrators of discipline, they were often hated more than the masters.'[8]

Lancashire Music-Making

Through these humble origins within the Lancashire cotton trade, Henry Watson was heir to a rich vernacular tradition of music. A biographical sketch in *Manchester Faces and Places*, written in 1894, states that his grandfather

> *had quite an envied reputation among the neighbourhood of Burnley; for he could play reasonably well any musical instrument that came his way. He especially distinguished himself with the bassoon, the clarinet, and the double bass. The apotheosis of music was achieved in*

those days at church and chapel anniversary services, at which, in the absence of an organ, an orchestra led the augmented choir, and sounded the praises of Zion from the eastern or western gallery. Joseph Watson was the hero of the best of these services; and the success of every such musical festival was known to be assured if his professional help had been secured to lead it.[9]

Henry's father was no less accomplished, playing the serpent and the trombone in the local band, and

one of the boy's earliest musical recollections (was) *holding cards of music in the street and at band practices for his father to play from, whereby Master Henry became a living music-desk.[10]*

Accrington in the 1850s

His father's occupation caused the family to move to Accrington, a growing town of which *Slater's Commercial Directory and Topography of Lancashire* (1856) recorded that 'the years 1852 and 1853 have been unprecedented, as regards the increase of cotton factories and population.' That population had reached 10,376 by the 1851 census, in which year Slater's suggested that,

it is within a comparatively few years that this district has obtained that importance which it now enjoys – this is attributable to its being the centre of the calico-printing business and surrounded also by cotton factories.[11]

Henry (Figure 4) attended Christ Church day school during which period of his life 'he was allowed to run wild, he hated school, and his surroundings were the very antithesis of culture.'[12]

Figure 4. Henry Watson at the age of eight. Published in the *Musical Times,* 1 June 1909. *Manchester Central Library.*

The physical nature of those early industrial surroundings was largely determined by the calico-printing entrepreneurs who shaped Accrington during its period of growth. Principal among these was the paternalistic Hargreaves family who controlled Broad Oak Printworks, established in 1792 in the wake of earlier local successes operated by the Peel dynasty. The influence of the Hargreaves family is clear from Mannex's *History, Topography and Directory of Mid-Lancashire.*

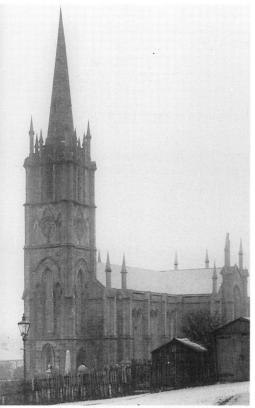

Figure 5. Christ Church, Accrington taken before 1954 when the steeples were taken down. *Lancashire County Council: Accrington Local Studies Library*

Christ's Church (Figure 5) *is a beautiful stone edifice in the early English style of architecture, erected in 1843 at a cost of £1,000, all raised by subscription, the Messrs Hargreaves of Broad Oak being the largest contributors.*[13]

Of Wellington Street itself (Figure 6), Richard Ainsworth stated in *Old Homesteads of Accrington* that it was built,

to facilitate the transit of goods between the New Factory and Broad Oak Works. Broad Oak Mill, still known as the 'New Factory', was built by the Hargreaves family; no wonder we hear the name of 'Factory Row' applied to Wellington Street.[14]

The mid-century appearance of the town (Figure 7) is documented in the Babbage Health Report of 1850. Remarking first that 'Accrington is situated in a deep valley, in the midst of a very hilly part of the county of Lancaster,' Babbage goes on to state that the main streets of the town are,

tolerably wide and regular, generally

Figure 6. Wellington Street, home for the young Henry Watson. *Lancashire County Council: Accrington Local Studies Library*

Figure 7. Accrington in 1848 on the first edition Ordnance Survey map (1:10560). Most of the development pre-1848 had been in the area between Abbey Street and the course taken by the railway line which opened in 1848. The Accrington to Preston line officially opened on 19 June 1848 to be followed shortly afterwards on 17 August by the Accrington to Stubbins and Bury extension and finally on 18 September by the Accrington to Burnley section.

well-paved, and have good footpaths running down both sides of them... The general aspect of the town is very clean, and justifies the boast of its inhabitants, that it is the cleanest town in Lancashire.[15]

The two principal streets seen by strangers passing through the town, namely Abbey Street and Blackburn Road, were distinguished by having houses faced with hewn stones, channelled roadways and underground drains. Free ventilation was attributable to the main streets being well laid out and to the town being positioned on what Babbage describes as an 'undulating surface.' Admittedly, the case was 'wholly reversed' in the unpaved yards, alleys and courts situated between and behind the main streets but, whatever may have been the nature of Henry Watson's immediate surroundings in the terraced rows of recently-built Wellington Street, the epithet 'antithesis of culture' cannot be applied to the entire town.

Accrington Music-Making

Henry's schooldays were not an entirely fallow period in his musical development. At the age of ten at Christ Church school,

(he) *gave promise of attaining a high position in the musical world (and) used to play the dulcimer at the Friday afternoon music lessons... and the children and teachers were delighted with his playing.*[16]

In his interview with the *Musical Times*, Dr Watson elaborated further on this period in his life.

I was about ten or eleven years old when I received the only pianoforte lessons I ever had. They were given me by Thomas Hargreaves, of revered memory, and a teacher – formerly an engraver – of Accrington, on an old square pianoforte of five octaves, which cost me less than £5. The fees, fifteen shillings a quarter, had to be scraped together somehow or other.[17]

The *Manchester Faces and Places* article acknowledged in 1894 the directing influence in this matter of Henry's father who 'at what the son now knows must have been pinching self-sacrifice... placed him under the tuition of Mr Hargreaves.'[18] Hargreaves is listed in the Accrington directories of this period as a teacher of music, resident at Ewbank Terrace on St James' Street. Also in the town, on Blackburn Road, was Enoch Bowker, a bookseller and stationer, printer, bookbinder, music and musical instrument seller, who was the principal organiser of a concert held in Accrington on 1 January

1841 which led to the formation of the Accrington Choral Society in 1842.[19]

Thus it can be seen that Henry Watson did not spend his formative years in a cultural desert, although the family's straitened circumstances forced him to earn a living as an accompanist.

> *At local fairs and functions I was paid seven and sixpence a night to play solos and accompaniments in public-houses, playing away till one o'clock in the morning, amid surroundings not the most refined. At those free-and-easy sing-songs I had to vamp the accompaniments and symphonies to the songs. A man would come up to me and say: 'Do you know so and so?' 'Ay,' I would answer in Lancashire fashion, and then we started off. Let me add that on Sundays the public-house music was always sacred!*[20]

Counselled by his grandfather to 'stick to music, Henry,' the future Dr Watson had found his niche.

> *He had by this time secured the reversion of his grandfather's reputation. He was proudly regarded by the good Accrington people as a sort of 'champion' extemporiser and accompanist. His youthful services were sought for popular concerts, and the Doctor is quite ready to admit that he owes a good deal to the practical and varied experiences of those boyhood's days.*[21]

Briefly, Henry boarded at the Mount Pleasant Academy on Whalley Road under the headship of Mr Broughton, at which institution he helped with the music in lieu of payment of fees. Meanwhile, he made astute use of the facilities offered at St James' Church, where he haunted the organ loft.

> *The organ, Master Henry proceeded with stolen opportunities to teach himself. On that instrument, indeed, Dr Watson states that he never had a professed lesson. Yet, before he was twelve years old, he had more than once taken the whole organ service at the Accrington Parish Church.*[22]

Panorama Show
The abrupt closure of Broughton's boarding school on the death of its founder led Henry to a situation as errand boy in a music shop recently opened in Blackburn. At the end of 1859, aged thirteen,

> *his wages were five shillings a week, out of which he had to pay his train fare daily from and to Accrington. His duties were to light the fires and sweep out the shop.*[23]

However, events soon took a startling turn when Henry was sought out by the proprietor of a travelling panorama show on American slavery. 'Box' Brown, a freed slave smuggled from Virginia to Philadelphia in a box, engaged Henry to provide a piano accompaniment to the changing scenes. For travelling with the show, he would receive £1 on top of travelling expenses. From Manchester, the show went through England to the Channel Islands, opening at Jersey in a large circus building on Easter Monday 1860. Dr Watson recalled that,

> *after three months in the Channel Islands we toured in Cornwall, the native county of Mrs Brown, to whose bonny little mulatto girl 'Uncle Harry', as I was always called, gave frequent lessons in the toddling art... But a new phase in my life was being rapidly prepared for me.* [24]

Dr Watson remembered of the show's sojourn in Manchester that it 'was the time of the cotton famine in Lancashire, and business was bad; but I was still able to send home some contributions to the household expenses.' [25]

The effects of the cotton famine led Edwin Waugh to note

> *the swarms of strange, shy, sad-looking singers and instrumental performers in the work-worn clothing of factory operatives who went about Manchester pleading for help in touching wails of simple song like so many wild birds driven by hard weather to the haunts of man.* [26]

Indeed, Dr Watson was so touched by the music of 'one of the many brass-bands of Lancashire operatives that tramped the country to raise the wind in a double sense during the cotton famine' that it made him feel homesick. [27]

It was just at this time that the recommendation of his former music master, Mr Hargreaves, secured him an apprentice's engagement with the firm of

Figure 8. Henry Watson at the age of fourteen. Published in *The Musical Times*, 1 June 1909. *Manchester Central Library.*

Edward Henry and Co of the Royal Exchange Arcade, Manchester. His apprenticeship began on New Year's Day, 1861, when he was still aged only fourteen (Figure 8).

> *I was to find my own food and clothing and to receive a wage of twelve shillings per week for the first year. I had a very varied experience during my four years' apprenticeship; tuning and repairing pianos and organs, showing off instruments, playing over songs and pieces to customers. I was much in request at concerts and entertainments . . . For a week at a time I used frequently to play at dance parties night after night, from eight p.m. to three or four o'clock in the morning. At this exhausting work, in hot rooms, I sometimes earned as much as £12 per week, one half of which dropped into my own slender pocket. But as I was then the practical mainstay of the household this extra pay for night work proved specially acceptable. I wanted to aim at something higher, but my circumstances then compelled me to keep at this lower level.*[28]

Doctorate

Those higher aspirations were fulfilled when Henry Watson, with a noted local teacher of singing, Henry Wilson, inaugurated the Manchester Vocal Society in 1867. Later that decade, his fortune was further assured when, assisted by Joseph Bracewell, he opened a music business in partnership with William Bracewell. Henry's attachment to the Bracewell family was reinforced by 'an interesting link in the relationship'[29] when Henry married Annie Maud Bracewell on 24 June 1874 at St Luke's Church in Cheetham Hill, Manchester (Figure 9).[30]

	When married	Name and surname	Age	Condition	Rank or profession	Residence at the time of marriage	Father's name and surname	Rank or profession of father
	1	2	3	4	5	6	7	8
291	June 24th 1874	Henry WATSON	Full	Bachelor	Music Seller	Stocks Farm Cheetham	Thomas WATSON	Mill Overlooker
		Annie Maud BRACEWELL	Full	Spinster	—	"	Joseph BRACEWELL	Grocer

Registration District Manchester

1874 MARRIAGE solemnized at the Parish Church

in the Parish of S. Luke Cheetham Hill in the County of Lancaster

Married in the Parish Church according to the Rites & Ceremonies of the Church of England by Banns by me,

Solemnized Henry Watson in the Joseph Bracewell   John Chippindale

between us Annie Maud Bracewell presence of us Jane HIGGIN William Hartley BRACEWELL   Rector

Figure 9. Copy of marriage certificate for Henry Watson and Annie Maud Bracewell 1874.

Astute copyright investments, sale of the land on which the shop stood at £84 per square yard in 1875, rapidly-increasing teaching engagements and a good pianoforte-tuning and repairing business consolidated Henry Watson's success. Accompanying a concert in Blackpool in 1878, he met a former fellow apprentice from his days at Henry & Co's Music Shop, Dr Henry Fisher, whose exercise for the degree of music was being performed in the town. Encouraged by Dr Fisher, Henry Watson secured his Bachelor of Music degree (Figure 10) from Cambridge in 1882 with a setting of the 103rd Psalm and, for his Doctor's degree in 1887, he submitted a sacred cantata *The Deliverance of Israel*. He later averred that

if he were allowed to include all he extemporised for the Accrington concerts and for the panorama tour, he would appear as one of the most prolific, as well as one of the most daring composers of the age... As a boy it was always music of a descriptive character which fascinated him; and he tells

Figure 10. Henry Watson in his degree robes, date uncertain. Taken by Mr Warwick Brookes, Manchester. Published in the *Musical Times*, 1 June 1909. *Manchester Central Library.*

of his returning, in those early days, from the fireworks at the Belle Vue Gardens, and thrashing his old square pianoforte almost out of shape, as well as out of tune, because it would not reproduce for him 'The siege of Algiers'.[31]

Dr Watson who, by his own admission, never had a singing-lesson in his life, was appointed professor of the Choral and Ear Training Department in the Royal Manchester College of Music on its opening in 1893, when the principal was Sir Charles Halle. He also lectured on musical history and instruments at Victoria University,

Manchester, held a series of church organist appointments and conducted numerous choral societies. In this latter capacity, his connection with Accrington was renewed towards the end of the century, when he conducted the Accrington Choral Society in a series of concerts at the Town Hall between 1896 and 1899. As well as two miscellaneous programmes, these included performances of the *Messiah*, Haydn's *Creation*, Gounod's *Faust*, Handel's *Samson* and Mendelssohn's *Elijah*. The Messiah concert was billed as having an 'orchestra selected from the members of the New Jerusalem Sunday School Band, assisted by leaders from Sir Charles Halle's orchestra.'[32]

A further indication that Dr Watson did not forget his Accrington roots is to be found in the first edition of his piano valse *Song Birds*, published by Henry & Co, on the front cover of which is printed the legend 'dedicated by permission to Mrs Thomas Hargreaves, Accrington.'

Legacy

On Tuesday 3 January 1911, Henry Watson died at 30 Chapel Street, Salford, his home of 40 years, after apparently being in his usual health on the previous Saturday. To casual observers, the end came suddenly, but Stanley Withers in an obituary tribute observed that,

> *only his intimate friends knew that for the last three years he had been carrying on his duties in the face of hopeless physical conditions, and that to his other virtues must be added that of unfailing courage.*[33]

The death notified to the registrar by J.A. Bracewell, his nephew present at the time of death, was certified as being caused by 'gastro hepatic carcinoma, four years' (Figure 11).[34]

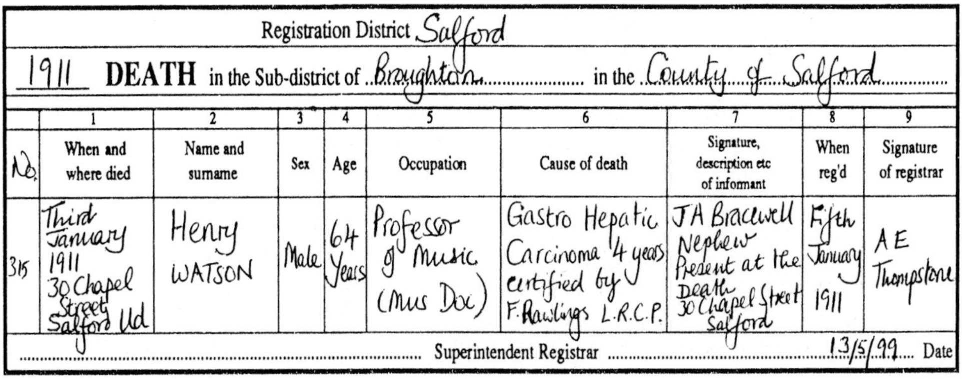

Registration District Salford

1911 DEATH in the Sub-district of Broughton in the County of Salford

	1	2	3	4	5	6	7	8	9
No.	When and where died	Name and surname	Sex	Age	Occupation	Cause of death	Signature, description etc of informant	When reg'd	Signature of registrar
315	Third January 1911 30 Chapel Street Salford Ud	Henry WATSON	Male	64 Years	Professor of Music (Mus Doc)	Gastro Hepatic Carcinoma 4 years certified by F. Rawlings L.R.C.P.	J A Bracewell Nephew Present at the Death 30 Chapel Street Salford	Fifth January 1911	A E Thompstone

Superintendent Registrar 13/5/99 Date

Figure 11. Copy of death certificate for Henry Watson 1911.

The Professor of Music was laid to rest at the Southern Cemetery in Manchester and on 25 January 1911 probate was granted to his widow, Annie Maud Watson, to administer the estate of £3961 16s 2d.[35]

Henry Watson's enduring public legacy remains his library, gifted to the Corporation of Manchester by a deed executed in 1899. This had been forecast in *Manchester Faces and Places* in 1894.

> *He hopes that the municipality, notwithstanding heavily pressing responsibilities, will do a little more for general musical education in the future than it has accomplished in the past; and he specially looks to it to see that the literature of music is more distinctly and more largely represented than at present, in the Manchester Free Reference Library. The smaller choral societies, he thinks, first languish and then die, from the difficulties which the cost of a continuous supply of music creates; and he considers that the educating, humanising, and moral influence of these societies is sufficient to justify any fostering care that the community might judiciously expend upon them. He would provide them with facilities for obtaining the loan of music free of cost, and we learn... that Dr Watson purposes giving the whole of his large and constantly growing musical library to one of the municipal or musical organisations of Manchester with this generous object in view.*[36]

To the *Accrington Observer and Times*, 'greater than these things, for those who knew him, was the simple kindliness and unpretentiousness of the man,'[37] whilst Stanley Withers paid tribute to 'a man of great sincerity of character and of unostentatious public spirit.'[38] Every year he had provided the music for a Sunday afternoon lecture in Ancoats, 'always happy to help good works without fee or reward of any kind.'[39] The Ancoats Recreation Movement was a socialist-inspired attempt to 'wean the majority of the working class of Ancoats away from the attractions of the pub and other commercially-based providers of working-class leisure.'[40] The last occasion on which Henry visited Ancoats, with a party of singers, took place only a month before he died.

His brother-in-law William Hartley Bracewell wrote,

> *it will be one of the grandest memories of 'Harry' Watson, as one could call him, that he was a Lancashire man... whose pride was ever in hailing and honouring the county as a pioneer of forward movements.*[41]

William paid affecting personal tribute to Henry as having 'entered with the enthusiasm of an elder brother into my plans and ambitions' and referred movingly to the bereft Annie Maud who had 'inspired the studies of young Harry Watson when he first came to Manchester.'[42]

In the *Millgate Monthly*, Gerald Cumberland described Henry Watson as,

> *a man of little above medium height, of spare frame, fine, broad and wrinkled forehead, and kindly eyes... He was the sanest and most genial man I have ever known... He was a piano-tuner and repairer, an actor, an accompanist, a trainer of choirs, a student, a teacher, a book-binder, a carpenter, a bibliophile, a music seller, an organiser of concerts, a composer, and many other things besides.*[43]

Accrington can proudly celebrate among her talented sons Dr Henry Watson, whose practical abilities, humanitarian qualities and commitment to the cause of universally accessible music education in his adopted city of Manchester, surely developed from his formative experiences in the town.

Acknowledgements

I would like to thank Manchester Central Library for assistance in providing me with three copies of photographs of Henry Watson from the *Musical Times*. I should also like to thank Lancashire County Council: Accrington Local Studies Library for kind permission to reproduce two photographs from their collection.

Notes and References

1 Birth certificate at the Henry Watson Music Library. Certificate summary sheet by Allen and Todd Stationers, Ramsbottom, Lancashire.
2 'Those who were illiterate made their marks, although there is some evidence that a mark did not always indicate illiteracy' – Pelling, George *Beginning Your Family History* 3rd ed 1984 p 27.
3 Henry Watson: the man, the books, the instruments *Musical Times*, 1 June 1909.
4 The late Dr Henry Watson: his connection with Accrington *Accrington Observer and Times*, 7 January 1911.
5 Lancashire Family History and Heraldry Society *1851 census surname index of Lancashire Vol 32: Haslingden and Accrington* 1987.
6 Computer-held index at Burnley Library.
7 Henry Watson, Mus Doc, Cantab *Manchester Faces and Places*, Vol 5, no 12, September 1894.
8 Aspin, Chris *The first industrial society: Lancashire: 1750-1850* Rev ed 1985 p 103.
9 *Manchester Faces and Places*, op cit.
10 *Musical Times*, op cit.
11 *Slater's Commercial Directory and Topography of Lancashire*, 1856.
12 *Musical Times*, op cit.
13 Mannex & Co *History, Topography and Directory of Mid-Lancashire*, 1854 p 391.
14 Ainsworth, Richard *Old Homesteads of Accrington : a series of 100 articles* 1917-19 No 72: Grange Farm.
15 Babbage, Benjamin Herschel *Report to the General Board of Health on a preliminary inquiry into the sewerage, drainage, and supply of water, and the sanitary condition of the inhabitants of the townships of New and Old Accrington in the County of Lancaster* 1850, p 5. Abbey, Warner, Oak, Blackburn,

Bank and Church Street were the main streets.

16 *Accrington Observer and Times*, op cit.

17 *Musical Times*, op cit.

18 *Manchester Faces and Places*, op cit.

19 Crossley, R.S. *Accrington Choral Society : historical sketch, 1842-92 : jubilee memento* 1892 p 2.

20 *Musical Times*, op cit.

21 *Manchester Faces and Places*, op cit.

22 Ibid.

23 *Musical Times*, op cit.

24 Ibid.

25 Ibid.

26 Aspin, op cit.

27 *Musical Times*, op cit.

28 Ibid.

29 Ibid.

30 Certificate obtained by postal application to the Family Records Centre following a search for the reference number in the microfilmed General Register Office indexes. Certificate summary sheet, op cit.

31 *Manchester Faces and Places*, op cit.

32 Accrington Choral Society *Concert Programmes and Annual Reports, 1890-99* Henry Watson Music Library.

33 *Manchester City News,* 7 January 1911.

34 Stomach and liver cancer. Death certificate obtained from Salford Register Office. Certificate summary sheet, op cit.

35 National probate calendars 1911 (microfiche).

36 *Manchester Faces and Places*, op cit.

37 *Accrington Observer and Times*, op cit.

38 *Manchester City News*, op cit.

39 *Accrington Observer and Times,* op cit.

40 Kay, Audrey *Charles Rowley and the Ancoats Recreation Movement*, 1876-1914, *Manchester Region History Review* Vol 7 1993 p 45-54.

41 *Manchester City News,* op cit.

42 Ibid.

43 Cumberland, Gerald *Dr Henry Watson: the musician and the man, Millgate Monthly* Vol 6, Part 1, February 1911.

7. ACCRINGTON NATURALLY

by Charles Gidman

ACCRINGTON NESTLES IN A BOWL-SHAPED HOLLOW
surrounded by hills (Figure 1). Highly distinctive terraced scenery
has evolved where the uplands appear as a series of stepped plateaux
rising from the valleys to the flat-topped hills. Erosion of shale
outcrops with their soft and crumbly consistency has resulted in hard
gritstone escarpments forming the hillcrests. There is widespread
evidence on the hilltops of large-scale quarrying of harder
sandstones, such as Dyneley Flag, Old Lawrence and Dandy Rock,
which has provided the setts and kerbstones characterising the
north-east Lancashire towns. Brickmaking, one of Accrington's
major industries, has exploited the younger rocks on the Coppice
and Whinney Hill which form the Accrington Mudstones. Thinly-
bedded rocks, once used for flagstones and roofing tiles before the
introduction of true slates, are also present.

Soil on these uplands is scarce but moorland vegetation is mixed,
with no particular plant dominant, except in localised areas. In
summer the moors are flecked with the white plumes of cotton grass
(Eriophorum angustifolium), which favours saturated conditions
and areas where erosion has taken place, enabling the development
of rhizomes (branching stems just below the soil surface). This
growth helps to stabilise the peaty environment and make it more
suitable for other grasses such as Purple Moor Grass (Molinia

Figure 1. 'View of Accrington', a painting showing a general view of the
town dated after 1848 with the newly opened railway viaduct to the left of
the picture. *Lancashire County Council: Accrington Local Studies Library*

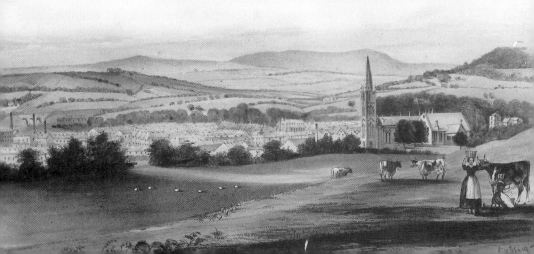

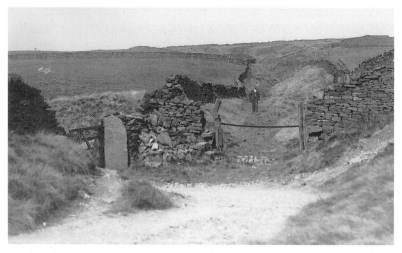

Figure 2. Rugged moorland surrounds the King's Highway, the original packhorse route between Clitheroe and Haslingden. It was recognized as the eastern boundary of the possessions held in Accrington by the monks of Kirkstall Abbey. On 22 April 1788, John Wesley travelled by this route from Padiham to Haslingden and complained that the roads were sufficient to lame any horse and shake any carriage to pieces. Time has not improved its condition! *Lancashire County Council: Accrington Local Studies Library*

caerulea), a decorative late spring flower. In late summer, the hillsides take on a purple hue with the flowering of the Wavy Hair-Grass (Deschampsia flexuosa). On a late autumn day, I have looked down upon an area of mixed moorland vegetation with a mosaic of colour provided by the various moorland sedges, rushes and grasses in their autumn finery. Truly a collection of individuals which belied their collective struggle for survival in such a hostile environment.

Although not as common as they once were, patches of yellow Bog Asphodel (Narthecium ossifragum) can still be seen in the district but insectivorous plants, normally associated with moorland bog flushes, are little represented in the area around Accrington. The moorland roll-call no longer includes small clumps of the Common Sundew (Drosera rotundifolia) in the wet sphagnum flushes and the Butterwort (Pinguicula vulgaris), but both were much more widespread some years ago. Heather and Bilberry are, however, well-established, the latter gaining territory every year, especially on the better drained slopes and ridges.

The skies above our hills are filled with the typical birds of a moorland scene: the Snipe, Lapwing, Wheatear and Pipit, along with the Curlew whose plaintive call can occasionally be heard.

Small mammals, such as Woodmice, Shrews and Voles, are widespread over the area as are moles which need a reasonably good depth of soil in which to operate their digging skills. Weasels can be glimpsed around their preferred habitats of old walls and derelict buildings but their cousin, the Stoat, is rarely seen. Rabbits are not so numerous now as they once were and the best time to see them is early in the morning or at dusk when they are out feeding. Foxes on the other hand are on the increase, growing much bolder, and can often be observed near homes on the edge of settlements.

It is virtually impossible now to visualize these surrounding areas of moorland (Figure 2), with their tussocky mounds and bog-pools, covered with extensive woodland. However, evidence of the remains of tree stumps and branches in the drainage channels, cut by moorland streams through the peat, indicate that this was indeed a wooded area, comprising mainly Birch trees with Sessile or Durmast Oak and Willow also quite widespread. Changes in climate causing the deposition of peat could have been a factor in the demise of the forest landscape. The area of Great Slack on Hameldon was used as a settlement site by neolithic people and later, after the Roman occupation, forest timber was used for charcoal burning, salt making, shipbuilding and other industries. Grazing animals throughout the centuries have then effectively prevented regeneration of the woodlands. The 1000 feet contour is the tree line for this area of north-east Lancashire today but, in some of the more remote higher areas of the district, Rowan trees still persist, their isolated position preventing the destruction of seedlings by animals.

Looking at the map of Hyndburn, woodland now appears to be widely scattered. Most of it is mixed woodland of broad-leaved species – Oak, Ash, Birch, Alder, Willow, Elm and Sycamore which, of course, is not a native tree. There are two conifer plantations in Great Harwood and Oswaldtwistle, maintained by the Forestry Commission, and smaller plantations in Altham and Accrington have been planted more recently.

What makes our woodlands interesting in relation to their flora is the complexity of varying habitats within a comparatively small area. We still have woodlands affectionately called 'Bluebell Woods', where the aspect is more open and Scrub Oak and Silver Birches proliferate, with ground cover provided by Soft Grass, Bluebells, Red Campion, Stitchwort, Buttercups, Bedstraw, Bracken and Fern. Huncoat, Altham and Rishton all have this type of woodland and, to a lesser extent, Accrington and Oswaldtwistle.

Figure 3. Warmden Falls, Accrington appreciated by two walkers around 1900. *Lancashire County Council: Accrington Local Studies Library*

Mention must be made of our distinctive cloughs (Figure 3), the deep-sided valleys where areas of scrubland in a transitional stage towards proper woodland create a home for a variety of plant and animal species different from their moorland neighbours. The spring brings cushions of Lesser Celandines (Ranunculus ficaria), Wood Anemones (Anemone nemerosa), Ransomes (Wild Garlic) and Red Campions (Silene dioica), all taking advantage of the available light filtering through leafless tree branches. Bluebells appear a little later and Brambles, Wild Roses, Guelder Roses and Elder all flourish. Heather, too, grows abundantly with Bilberry and Bracken. Additional colour is provided during the summer months by flowers such as Brooms (Cytisus scoparius), Bird's-Foot Trefoil (Lotus corniculatus), other Vetches (Vicia), Sneezewort (Achillea ptarmica), Hawkweeds (Hieracium) and Tormentil (Potentilla erecta). Vigorous seedlings of trees, such as catkin-bearing Alders, Willows, Birch and Elm, have also found hospitable conditions in this landscape. Woodland areas should be visited at different times during the growing season to appreciate the colour and variety of their flora.

A recent introduction to this area is the Grey Squirrel; this species arrived in the British Isles between 1876 and 1929 during which time it repeatedly escaped from captivity. Since then it has spread to a large part of the country and ousted the native Red Squirrel. It is a serious pest, a good swimmer, a very able climber jumping up to

Figure 4. Laund Clough, Accrington 1990s. A photograph taken in a northern town which belies the stereotypical image of a smoke-blackened, ugly industrial area. *Lancashire County Council: Accrington Local Studies Library*

twelve feet, and eats a great variety of food. Bulbs, roots, tree-bark, cones, nuts, fungi, grain and birds' eggs are all consumed in their endless quest for food. I mention these details in the hope that it may deter people from feeding these skilled hunters which are responsible, along with a growing imbalance of predators, for reducing the number of our smaller song birds in the cloughs.

The cloughs are also a sanctuary for larger birds with my local wildlife haunt, Laund Clough (Figure 4), supporting Jays, Ring Doves, Greater Spotted Woodpeckers, Tawny Owls and the more common and noisy Rooks, Crows and Magpies.

Although it often seems that Hyndburn receives more than its fair share of rainfall, especially during the very wet and mild winter of 1998-1999, the mean rainfall for 1994-1998 was still only around the average of 44.96 inches per year. Some areas of water have been lost, however, with the culverting of ponds and streams and even the draining of reservoirs, but places remain where these freshwater habitats have been encouraged.

On larger areas of water, such as mill lodges and the rivers Hyndburn and Calder, plant life has adapted to watery conditions in different ways. Plants familiar to us as 'pondweeds', such as Canadian Pondweed, are totally submerged. Other species, although mostly submerged, do present leaves and flowers on the water surface as in the Crowfoots, whose white buttercup-like flowers cover the stream surface in July and August, eg on Woodnook Water. Other aquatic species of plants, such as Water Plantain (Alisma plantago-aquatica), Bur-reed (Sparganium) and Arrowhead (Sagittaria sagittifolia), are rooted in the silt and grow up to flower above the surface of the water.

Along the margins of slow-flowing rivers and canals, a plant species may become so successful that it will completely take over the whole area; an example of this is the Reed-Grass growing near the disused coke ovens at Church.[1] This is a fringe reed-swamp area and the Great Reedmace (Bulrush), with a good mix of Sedges, Rushes and Reed-grasses, creates a swampy area. This forms a halfway stage between aquatic plants and marsh.

With continual die-back from successive generations of plants, the organic humus builds up in time to give marsh conditions. Only a brief step is needed to produce a situation where mineral matter becomes mixed in with organic plant remains, making a suitable substrate for a wide range of plants to grow successfully on the edge of rivers and streams as marginal flora. This condition is appreciated by species such as: Brooklime (Veronica beccabunga); Gipsy-Wort (Lycopus europaeus); Meadow-Sweet (Filipendula ulmaria); Sweet Flag (Acorus calamus); and Common Skull-Cap (Scutellaria galericulata). The Himalayan Balsam (Impatiens glandulifera) should be mentioned as one such plant which is established in our local cloughs and especially along river margins. Although an annual, it grows several feet in height and hybridises freely, producing a range of purple-red-pink-white flowers and is capable of resisting heavy pollution without mishap.

The rural areas are not alone in their wealth of plant life. In early summer in our towns, especially where development projects are taking place, one can see evidence of how quickly pockets of dereliction can become populated with plants. One of the earliest plants, Coltsfoot (Tussilago farfara), thrives on rough land, but is usually elbowed out by other more prolific species, such as: Shepherd's Purse (Capsella bursa-pastoris); Mugwort (Artemisia vulgaris); Chick-weed (Stellaria media); Plantain (Plantago major); Dandelion (Taraxacum vulgaria); Broadleaved Dock (Rumex obtusifolius); Rosebay Willow-Herb (Chamaenerion angustifolium); and Common Sow-Thistle (Sonchus asper). Plants are opportunists and one now firmly established in Accrington over recent years is the Oxford Ragwort (Senecio squalidus). Sicilian in origin, this plant was first recorded in Oxford in 1794 and has spread vigorously from there, possibly along the route of the Great Western Railway. It is prevalent now in south Accrington and with its deep, golden-yellow daisy-like flowers can be seen along with its cousin, the Groundsel (Senecio vulgaris), for most of the year.

However, it is the invertebrates which I find fascinating. In 1945, Kloet and Hincks[2] listed over 20,000 species known to occur in the British Isles and even now new species are being added to this total. The more familiar orders of insects include: Bumble Bees, Earwigs, Lacewings, Froghoppers, Ants, Grasshoppers and the multitude of creatures which spend most of their lives in water, later emerging as adults – Dragon-flies, Stone-flies, Common Pond Skaters, Water Boatmen and the curious Caddis-Flies, known for their peculiar tubular cases which house their pupae.

Figure 5. Drawing of a male and female Orange-tip on a foodplant Mayflower from an original watercolour by the author and printed as a notelet by Springvalley Services, Darwen. *Author's collection*

My own particular interest is the Lepidoptera – butterflies and moths. I can take this opportunity to report on the status of the species on the local scene. There are 56 species of butterflies in the British Isles, seventeen of which have been noted in the Hyndburn area. Several are well-known: Small Tortoiseshell (Aglais urticae); Large White (Pieris brassicae); and the Red Admiral (Vanessa atalanta). The latter does not over-winter here so those observed before the end of May or June are possible arrivals from Europe where they, and another immigrant, the Painted Lady (Cynthia cardui) are frequently seen. A butterfly which has become a breeding species here during recent years is the Orange Tip (Anthocharis cardamines), only the male of which wears the orange colour (Figure 5). The lovely Peacock butterfly (Inachis io) is now also breeding in the area (Figure 6). The visit of a Comma butterfly (Polygonia c-album) to my garden on 19 August 1998 was a truly memorable occasion (Figure 7), for this was a new species to the district and its sighting compensated for the lack of butterfly activity throughout that summer due to inclement

Figure 6. Peacock butterfly (Inachis io), new to Hyndburn, taken in 1995. *Author's collection*

conditions. There are colonies of the Common Blue (Polyommatus icarus) in Huncoat and Rishton and the Holly Blue (Celastrina argiolus) has often been observed in Clayton-le-Moors. Global warming may result in several butterfly species on the wing in December even in the north of England.

Recent improvements in the natural surroundings of the Hyndburn area have not been accidental. The achievements at Foxhill Bank Nature Reserve in Oswaldtwistle are nothing less than spectacular in providing an oasis of peacefulness within an urban community. This well-wooded reserve is managed by the Lancashire Wildlife Trust through their site warden[3] [see Chapter 10 for the report of a visit by Prince Charles to the reserve. Ed]. Tinker Brook is now clean enough to attract a pair of Kingfishers and Dippers with Tawny Owls breeding there regularly.

As long ago as 1970, however, there were plans to return part of Accrington to its former glory. As a teacher of Environmental Studies at Holy Family RC Secondary School, now Mount Carmel, I was trying to organise a school project with a suitable theme to mark Conservation Year. I arranged to meet Mr Till, the

Figure 7. Comma butterfly (Polygonia c-album), also a new visitor in the area, taken in author's garden, 19 August 1998. *Author's collection*

Superintendent of Parks in Accrington, to discuss a project to plant trees on the Coppice, which, at that time, was devoid of any kind of shrub, bush or tree, in contradiction to its name (Figure 8). Mr Till agreed to provide tree-seedlings with the necessary larch poles and sheep netting for protection and I volunteered a week's labour from ten fifth year students to help juniors from local schools plant the seedlings on the Coppice. The species chosen were Alder, Willow, Scots' Pine, Thorn, Birch and Sitka Spruce. Eight sites were selected and 1,600 seedlings were planted. Extra hands were welcome and Accrington College sent 20 students to assist other helpers from St Christopher's C of E School. This gargantuan project was completed on 24 March 1970 with the assistance of Mr T. Haworth and Mr Michael Baines from Chorley College who filled the last site on the

Figure 8. Looking up to a Coppice bereft of trees from the top of Avenue Parade, Accrington. The photograph was taken before the facilities of Peel Park were opened in 1939. The 'white horse' scar near the summit of the Coppice has only recently been partially disguised by the fast growing trees which now clothe the sides of the hill. *Lancashire County Council: Accrington Local Studies Library*

Coppice. Now, 30 years later, there is once again a new 'aspect of Accrington', a tree-covered Coppice.

To my knowledge, there has been no survey undertaken on the effect of these trees on the environment and any resulting increase in both plant and animal life. There is an urgent need for a listing of the flora and fauna of the whole Hyndburn area so that, over time and if monitored, the pattern of survival for many different species could be assessed. A group of enthusiastic volunteers, selecting their own particular sphere of interest in natural life forms, could undertake such a project, possibly under the auspices of a newly created Hyndburn Conservation and Recording Society. Calling all interested natural historians!

Acknowledgements

I would like to thank Lancashire County Council: Accrington Local Studies Library for kind permission to reproduce several photographs from their collection in this article. Thanks are also due to Mr Denis Cassidy, headteacher of Mount Carmel School, who marked Conservation Year, 1970 with a full week's school work with conservation in mind which included help with The Coppice Planting Scheme.

Notes and References

1 The extensive ruins of the beehive coke ovens next to the Leeds & Liverpool canal are the remains of Aspen Colliery developed in 1868-69 by Thomas Simpson and Company.
2 Kloet, G. Sydney and Hincks, Walter Douglas *Checklist of British Insects etc*, Kloet and Hincks, Stockport, 1945.
3 At the time of writing, Stuart Nokes is the warden of Foxhill Bank Nature Reserve.

8. WITH INJUSTICE AND OPPRESSION I MAKE NO COMPROMISE: THE EASTER DUES QUESTION

by Catherine Duckworth

THE CHURCH OF ENGLAND, as the established church in this country, has claimed numerous rights over individuals, some of which have been challenged over the centuries. Accrington was at the forefront of one of these conflicts; its cause, as in so many cases, centred on money.

The Rubric at the end of the Communion Service as laid down in the 1662 Prayer Book says,

> *and yearly at Easter every Parishioner shall reckon with the Parson, Vicar or Curate, or his or their Deputy or Deputies, and pay to them or him all Ecclesiastical Duties, accustomably due, then and at that time to be paid.*

It was over the interpretation of these words that problems ensued. The key elements which were to be challenged were 'every parishioner' and 'accustomably due'.

It is important to understand the difference between Easter offerings and Easter dues. The former comprises that which is given on the plate on Easter Sunday. It supplements the income of the benefice and is a direct gift to the clergy paid by the congregation and, as such, carries a strong element of free will. Easter dues, however, were payable by every householder for each member of his family aged over sixteen years; the amount varied according to the custom of the place, but was usually around tuppence per head. This, of course, amounted to a poll tax, never popular with the English, and even tuppence per head could be punitive where incomes were very low. For many years there were few problems as the vast majority of the population supported the established church but, as time went on and the nonconformist movement gained ground, there developed resistance to paying money to the Church of England.

In Accrington there were also complications over to whom the money was paid. The Vicar of Whalley claimed payment by ancient right, although the town was in the parish of Accrington, of the chapelry of Altham. It was collected by an agent of the Vicar of Altham but, by the nineteenth century, Accrington had much outgrown its neighbour Altham, whose industry had diminished as

Figure 1. The ancient Parish Church of St Mary and All Saints, Whalley. The foundation and the building both long predate the Abbey founded adjacent to it by the monks of Stanlaw. It was the mother church of an ancient and very extensive parish. *Lancashire County Council: Accrington Local Studies Library*

described by Mike Clarke in Chapter 5, CANAL WORKERS AND BOATMEN AROUND ACCRINGTON' Whalley (Figure 1), five miles and several parishes away, seemed very remote, all of which contributed to the feelings of resentment. To understand the whole story it is necessary to consider the history of the Church of England in this area.

The ancient Parish of Whalley, from the time of its Saxon foundation, extended over 161 square miles. It actually covered one ninth of the area of the County of Lancashire (pre 1974) or, in other words, the entire area of the post 1974 boroughs of Pendle, Burnley and Hyndburn, part of Rossendale and most of Ribble Valley. An inquisition, taken at Whalley in 1650, listed the seventeen chapelries which were to be created out of the one, including three from the Accrington area. These were Accrington, Altham covering Altham and Clayton-le-Moors (Figure 2), and Church Kirk, covering

Church, Oswaldtwistle, Huncoat and part of Clayton-le-Moors. The ministers of Altham and Church Kirk each received £10 from the rectory and £30 from the county commissioners. The stipend of the Vicar of Whalley was to be £38 from Mr Thomas Assheton.

It can be seen from this that the stipend of the Vicar of Whalley was not very generous, particularly if viewed in the context of the neighbouring parishes of Rochdale and Blackburn. These had received much greater endowments following the dissolution of the monasteries and, accordingly, had much higher incomes. By the mid eighteenth century, the value of the stipend had been further eroded, the nonconformist movement had grown, the common man was beginning to receive more education and to wish to take more control of his own destiny. These combined to create a volatile situation, which reached a climax in Accrington in 1860.

The Vicar of Whalley, the Reverend R.N. Whitaker, was trying to raise income from every possible source and pursued the Easter dues

Figure 2. St James Church, Altham in about 1860. The tower was built in 1859 and the stonework appears fresh. The stove pipe hat of the man in the foreground is also of that period. *Lancashire County Council: Accrington Local Studies Library*

with vigour. The dues in Accrington were collected through the offices of the Vicar of Altham, but it was decided that for legal purposes the claim was through the Vicar of Whalley. Realising that certain individuals had refused to pay, he decided to make an example of them. He issued summonses against John Newton and John Massey for non-payment of eleven pence each, that is, 5¹/₂d each for two years' Easter dues. Much was made throughout all the court hearings of the small amount of money at issue. Apart from the principle at stake, however, 5¹/₂d per annum multiplied by the adult population of the whole ancient parish amounted to the very large sum of £569 8s 4d. In Accrington alone, following the expansion in the population caused by the industrial revolution, the amount had risen from £12 6s 7d in 1801, to £43 4s 8d in 1851 and £60 9s 2d in 1860 and was still rising fast. To the poor, however, 5¹/₂d could represent the difference between food and hunger. There was no element of means testing since all were expected to pay. There was a case of an elderly woman on 6d poor relief per week having to pay 5d of the six for the dues. The court case united the populace against a common foe.

The *Preston Guardian* of 21 July 1860 carried the following notice

Figure 3. Charles 'Torney' Hall lived in *Gothic Cottage*, St James' Street. Always active in town and church life, he became one of Accrington's characters. *Lancashire County Council: Accrington Local Studies Library.*

> *Easter Dues – On Wednesday the bellman made the following novel announcement:- 'Notice! This is to inform the inhabitants of Accrington that they must not pay any Easter dues as several gentlemen of the town are forming an Anti-Easter Due Association. By order of the Committee.'*

This is placed immediately above a detailed and very partisan report of a prosecution for the recovery of Easter dues. This marks the beginning of the many court cases of the Vicar of Whalley versus various townspeople and reports that, at the petty sessions, John Newton and John Massey were summoned for the non-payment of 11d, the debt for two years' Easter dues. It was obviously a David and Goliath contest, with John Massey, schoolmaster of the

Figure 4. Reverend Charles Williams. This photograph was taken in his venerable old age, although the court case was during his first period of ministry in Accrington. His long and influential service to the town commenced in July 1851. He was always ready to speak out about his strong principles and had a great deal of influence at a formative time. *Lancashire County Council: Accrington Local Studies Library.*

Swedenborgian (or New Jerusalem) School, attempting to mount his own defence against the Reverend R.N. Whitaker, who was backed by the Vicars of Altham and Church Kirk, and represented by Charles Hall, attorney, of Accrington (Figure 3). John Newton did not appear, claiming to be away from home both when the summons was served and on the occasion of the court case. The near verbatim reporting brings the court to life, with John Massey giving a good account of himself, despite his obvious social disadvantage which Charles Hall took every opportunity to impress upon him.

Mr Hall set the scene by referring to the various Acts of Parliament and old deeds which he was using to pursue the case and called upon the Vicar of Whalley to give evidence, saying that the defendant was at liberty to ask any questions. At this point the proceedings appeared to descend into farce as Mr Massey asked questions such as 'Under what statute is the claim founded?' Mr Hall immediately instructed the vicar not to answer that question and proceeded to do the same with every question put by the defendant. There was laughter amongst the crowd when Mr Hall said that he 'objected to such questions; they are not proper ones and they are put in such an uncouth mode'. Mr Massey had had the temerity to enquire about what service the vicar had done for him that he should pay for it. It would seem to us to be a reasonable request. Mr Hall took the same stance when the next witness, Mr Wilkinson the collector, who was also the schoolmaster at the National School at Altham, was called. Despite all Mr Massey could do, the presiding magistrate ruled that the defendant was ordered to pay the full amount due but could appeal.

The leader writers were convinced that the anti-Easter dues camp would prevail. The voters of the Ribble Valley, which includes

Whalley, helped bring about the downfall of the poll tax in the late twentieth century. In comments foreshadowing this, the *Preston Guardian* writer said,

> *should the movement be successful, we shall thus be furnished with an example of a community freeing themselves by their own act from an oppressive exaction, without having to resort to arms.*

It is interesting to see the role of the dissenting ministers in this. The collectors had been told not to collect from them, so they could have kept out of the matter as did the Roman Catholic clergy. Clergymen such as Reverend Charles Williams, Baptist minister (Figure 4), and Reverend Joseph Haley, the Independent minister, decided to support their congregations and a public meeting was called. The *Accrington Free Press* of 21 July 1860 carried a letter from 'Free-Will Offering' exhorting the people to attend a public meeting. The same issue also carried an advertisement for the same meeting to be held on vacant ground near Park Shed. The meeting was, however, apparently transferred to the Peel Institution (Figure 5). Men of Accrington were asked 'to prove by their presence that these Easter dues are... odious, obnoxious, and unjust!' There is also a letter from Reverend R.N. Featherston, the Vicar of Christ Church, Accrington, stating his agreement to serving on the committee of the Anti-Easter

Figure 5. The Peel Institution was opened on 24 December 1858. It was originally built as a memorial to Sir Robert Peel and it included Assembly Rooms which quickly became the centre for social life in the area. It was also the early home, at different times, of the Mechanics' Institution, the Post Office and the Library. *Lancashire County Council: Accrington Local Studies Library.*

Dues Association. The provisos were that the collection should not be made until the end of Mr Sharp's incumbency at Altham and that it should free dissenters from payment. In the event, his name does not appear again. The Anti-Easter Dues Association, thus formed, adopted the motto of the recently opened Peel Institution as their own. The bust of Peel, which faced the crowds flocking to the Assembly Room at the head of the stairs, still bears the inscription 'With injustice and oppression I make no compromise'.

The newspapers gave unfailing support to the underdog throughout the contest, although the *Accrington Free Press* ceased publication on the eve of the court case of 1 September 1860, much to the dismay of the editor. Until this time, the editor, Mr Bowker, not only reports events in partisan spirit, but also takes an active role in the meetings.

The *Guardian* of the 28 July 1860 reports that,

> *one of the largest public meetings which has ever been held in Accrington took place in the Peel Institution, the object being to consider the* (Easter due) *question. The room was literally crammed though not a single bill had been posted to announce the meeting.*

Although numbers are not given, other meetings held around that time at the Peel Institution attracted over 1,000, so we can assume at least that number attended.

The *Accrington Free Press* reported that resistance so far had been 'quiet and amusing', with one person requesting that the vicar collected the money himself and another giving a banker's order for 5½d. The *Preston Guardian*, in a supplement on the 28 July 1860, reports in detail the public meeting of the previous Monday, over which Mr Entwistle, draper, was called upon to preside. On the platform were Reverend Charles Williams, Baptist minister, Reverend J. Haley, Independent minister, Reverend A. Haworth, Swedenborgian minister, Mr Thomas Tattersall, Mr Bowker[1], Mr J. Swain, Mr Pollard and others.

John Massey was first to address the gathering and concluded by reading this resolution:

> *that in the opinion of this meeting Easter dues are an unjust and vexatious impost, and that, therefore, all legal and practical measures should be adopted to abolish them.*

Over the following months this was indeed what happened. Reverend J. Haley, seconding the resolution, said that he 'considered it a piece of ecclesiastical tyranny... nonetheless so because as his lawyer said it had the sanction of the law'.

The Anti-Easter Dues Association had been well and truly launched, with considerable foresight. It was immediately very well organised. It had obviously been realised that a united front would have more chance of success. The members contributed to the fund which was used to pay counsel and also to buy back goods removed by bailiffs and sold by auction. A further report in the *Preston Guardian Supplement* of 28 July 1860 told of the town having been divided into districts by the association and how funds and members were being canvassed. Seven hundred householders had agreed to pay no more. Then in a ludicrous vignette the following was reported;

> *The individual who collects the obnoxious impost, in going his round on Wednesday last in a street in Accrington, was furiously assailed by a crowd of women, who jeeringly demanded "what he wanted 5¹/₂d for?" The crowd increased, and the collector finding a storm brewing which was very likely to burst upon him, made his collecting book safe, buttoned his coat as though bent [sic] jumping over the heads of everybody in the street, and with a hop, skip and jump, he bounced into a house, out of the back door in a second, with his assailants close upon him, and in at the back door of another house, where he craved that they would throw a shield of protection over him until he recruited his strength. After staying inside for a short time he took to his heels, and the last time he was seen he was going over hedge and ditch to Altham where it is hoped he will tarry.*

The leader writer of the *Accrington Free Press* of 28 July 1860 was particularly struck by the role the women could play, which he felt was reminiscent of the women of France opposing Louis XVI.

> *When women condescend to fight, conquest is easy to them. The question is settled. And, if we mistake not, the determination of our wives not to pay will do more than the eloquent exposition of Nonconformity by Mr Haley, the calm reasoning of Mr Tattersall…,the practical suggestions of Mr Williams, or even the heroic stand made by Messrs Massey and Newton. The question is decided: for when women say they won't, they won't, and there's an end of it. Easter dues are doomed.*

Unfortunately, this took a little more time than expected.

By the time of the special session of the county magistrates at Court House, Accrington (Figure 6), reported on 1 September 1860, the Association had 1,200 members. The next trial was against

Figure 6. The Court House, Manchester Road was erected in 1835. Accrington Local Board held their first meeting here in 1853, the police court was held here, with the prisoners' cells in the basement. It was later used by Congregationalists, Unitarians, and then Catholic Apostolics who occupied it for many years. It was demolished in 1931 under the *Accrington Improvement Act*. The adjoining shop premises were the offices for the Magistrate's Clerk. *Lancashire County Council: Accrington Local Studies Library*

John Newton alone, supported by his counsel paid for by the Association. The Quarter Sessions of the 20 October 1860 heard the case of the Vicar of Whalley v John Newton. The said John Newton had refused to pay 11d, due and payable to the Reverend R.N. Whitaker. The case commenced at 11.00am and lasted until 5.10pm. A verbatim report of the trial was published in the *Preston Guardian* and was also later printed as a pamphlet which gives a flavour of the proceedings. There was great detail about the historical basis and much about legal precedent. There was also a considerable semantic discussion concerning the words 'offering', 'oblation' and 'obvention'. Exemption was claimed from the operation of the *Tithes Commutation Act*. It was stated that it had been the custom in the Parish of Whalley to pay what is commonly called a house debt, amounting to $4^1/2$d and then $^1/2$d for each communicant. It is rather surprising that the prosecution case should use 'communicant' here.

The rubrics clearly state 'parishioner' and this would have been far easier to prove. The main crux of the defence case was that the nonconformists were not, and could not be, communicants. John Newton should, according to the counsel, have paid 4^1/$_2$d for the house and ^{1}/$_2$d each for himself and his wife, making 5^1/$_2$d, and, since this was due for two years, the debt was 11d. The collector, Thomas Wilkinson, gave evidence of going to try to collect dues from John Newton on 16 June and again on 10 July. The collections were made according to a ledger which detailed the amount collected the previous year. Some of the collectors also collected from those aged over fourteen. There was also evidence that the clergy had in the past collected for a cow (1^1/$_2$d), plough (1d), hay (1d), lamb (1d), sheep, sold (1d), foal (1d), swarm of bees (1d), bull (2d), stallion (2d), but it was the custom just to claim 4^1/$_2$d house debt and ^{1}/$_2$d per communicant to the limit of 5^1/$_2$d.

The case for the defence put forward cogent arguments, with great debate about the meaning of 'communicant' in the rubrics of the Prayer Book. The Church said that, by common practice, this referred to everyone over the age of sixteen; the nonconformists argued that it only included those who shared the Lord's Supper in the Anglican Church. As dissenters were not confirmed members of the Church of England, they could not be admitted to Communion. There was also much made of the differing amounts of money collected for different clergy, some demanding ^{1}/$_2$d per head, others more. After careful debate and, just as another witness was to be called, the judge said that he had heard enough and that the prosecution case was proven. Costs were awarded against the defendants as the judge considered that a man should not have to go to the higher courts over 11d and, rather abruptly, the court rose. To the modern reader, the case seems as well proven for the defence as it did to the newspapers of the time. The law, however, sided with the Established Church.

This was not to be accepted quietly and the Anti-Easter Dues Association immediately convened a 'public indignation meeting.' This was 'to give ratepayers an opportunity of recording their protest against a tax which they considered to be "one of those flagrant wrongs calling aloud for redress".' Many hundreds of people again made their way to the Peel Institution and soon after eight o'clock on the Wednesday following Saturday's Assizes the Reverend Charles Williams introduced Mr Midgeley to chair the meeting. The latter likened the townspeople to the Italians in their desire for freedom. 'He hoped they would be as ready and as numerous as the volunteers who had gone forth to assist Garibaldi'. There were many stirring words spoken, rousing the populace and encouraging them to stand firm. Reverend Charles Williams spoke at length and said that the committee was resolved

> *to organise a moral resistance to the unjust demand of the Vicar of Whalley by solemnly declaring its determination to suffer distraint rather than pay the Easter dues.*

Williams told of steps that were being taken to take the debate beyond Accrington. Already the support of the Society for the Liberation of Religion from State Patronage and Control had been offered and there were hopes that a bill would soon be offered in Parliament to abolish the dues.

The men of Accrington continued to refuse to pay and distress warrants were issued in due course; on Monday 10 December 1860, six boots taken from John Newton and three watches taken from Mr Cronshaw were sold by public auction. The goods were bought by members of the association and paid for out of the funds. The auctions took place on more than one occasion as different men were taken to court. At one point Charles Williams had to intervene as the mood of the crowd became so ugly the auctioneer feared for his life. The people were persuaded to go to the market place where a further meeting was held. By this time 2,000 men in Accrington were prepared to make the stand and refuse payment; and the case was being discussed throughout the country. Rossendale, Preston and other towns all joined the fray. The *Christian Spectator* published a lengthy condemnation by C.W., probably Charles Williams, which was printed and generally released in February 1861; he waited until June 1861 before preaching on the subject and this was also published. He took as his text 1 Samuel, chapter 2, verse 16 'Thou shalt give it me now; and if not I will take it by force'.

Wylie in his history of *The Baptist Churches of Accrington and District* records that there was a local ballad composed at that time. There were four verses and chorus, the latter of which is now the sole survivor,

> *Hammer and tongs they fired away,*
> *And words like bullets flew,*
> *Nine out of ten refused to pay*
> *Any Easter Due.*

For two years the battle was fought until the clergy quietly ceased to demand their dues. Other towns followed their example. The

Magistrate's Clerk drew the Home Secretary's attention to what was happening in Accrington, the question was brought before Parliament and compulsory Easter dues were abolished throughout the country.

Acknowledgements

My thanks to Lancashire County Council: Accrington Local Studies Library for permission to use photographs from the collection and to the present Vicar of Whalley, the Reverend Christopher Sterry, for his knowledgeable support and encouragement whilst writing this article.

Further Reading

Whitaker, Thomas Dunham *An History of the Original Parish of Whalley and the Honor of Clitheroe*, Routledge, 4th ed, 1872
Accrington Free Press, 21 July 1860
Accrington Free Press, 24 July 1860
Accrington Free Press, 18 August 1860
Accrington Free Press, 25 August 1860
Accrington Free Press, 1 September 1860
Preston Guardian, 1 September 1860
Preston Guardian Supplement, 27 October 1860
The Vicar of Whalley, R.N. Whittaker [sic][2], v John Newton, Accrington. *A Full Report of the Easter Due Case, heard at the Quarter Sessions, Preston, on the 20th October, 1860 before T.B. Addison and Peter Catterall Esqrs*, Toulmin, nd.
Easter Dues, weighed in the balances of the sanctuary: a sermon preached in the Accrington Road Chapel, Accrington on Sunday evening, June 30, 1861, by the Reverend Charles Williams. Published by request.
Easter Offerings: a Lancashire Story reprinted from the *Christian Spectator*, February 1861
Wylie, R.J.V. *The Baptist Churches of Accrington and District*, 1923

Notes and References

1 The Mr Bowker referred to here was most likely one of the newspaper family, who then reported on the event in the *Accrington Free Press*.
2 Reverend R.N. Whitaker, whose name should be spelt with one 't', invariably had his name misspelt in the newspapers and other publications of the time

9. ACCRINGTON STANLEY: A BRIEF HISTORY

by Jean Harrison

ONE CANNOT BEGIN TO WRITE a history of Accrington
Stanley without first mentioning their predecessors, Accrington FC,
who eventually were to become one of the founder members of the
Football League. Affectionately known as 'Th'Owd Reds',
Accrington FC was formed c1876. In 1878 a public meeting was
held at the *Black Horse* pub in Abbey Street to decide whether the
team should play Association Football or Rugby. A committee was
duly elected with Colonel Hargreaves appointed as president and it
was decided that the club would play Association Football and its
colours would be scarlet shirts and black shorts.

During their first season, Accrington shared a ground on
Thorneyholme Road with Accrington Cricket Club and on 28
September 1878 they played their first game against Church Rovers,
which they won by a disputed goal. Two matches were played under
'floodlights' during this first season, the first one being against
Blackburn Rovers at Alexandra Meadows on 4 November 1878
when Accrington were beaten 4-0, one of which was also a disputed
goal. A 'Gramme' light was attached to a pole about 40 feet high at
either end of the ground, giving off a light equivalent to c6000 candle
power. It was necessary to paint the ball white in order to see it. The
other match to be played under 'floodlights' was a 3-3 draw against
Church.

In 1879-80 the Lancashire Cup was established, a trophy which
Accrington were to win three times. Their first success came in 1881
when Accrington played Blackburn Park Road in the final at Darwen
and won the game 6-4. In 1888 one of the most unusual matches in
football was to involve Accrington in their second Lancashire Cup
Final. Their opponents in the final that year were to be Preston
North End, who were unhappy about the venue chosen for the final,
Ewood Park, claiming that it was too close to Accrington. The
Lancashire Football League were determined that the final should go
ahead and advertised the match as Accrington versus Preston North
End, but made alternative arrangements with Witton Football Club,
as losing semi-finalists, to step in should Preston fail to turn up.
Preston did not turn up for the match and so the Accrington team

Figure 1. Stanley in action at their Moorhead Ground c1910. *Lancashire County Council: Accrington Local Studies Library*

took to the field alone, kicked off and George Haworth duly scored a goal. The referee immediately ended the match, declaring Accrington the winners and they were presented with the trophy. The alternatively scheduled match against Witton then followed, when Accrington were defeated 4-0. Accrington won the Lancashire Cup for a third time during the following season 1888-89 when they beat Higher Walton in the final 1-0 after a replay.

In 1882 the cricket club agreed to let Accrington play on the south west side of their Thorneyholme Road Ground and the football club were given permission to build a stand. The following year, however, they were ordered to remove the stand after every match!

In 1883 Accrington were in trouble with the Football Association when they were accused of playing a professional player, James Beresford, and the club was subsequently expelled by the FA. However, after much unrest in Lancashire following this decision, the FA decided in December to re-instate Accrington as a member of the English Football Association, but they were not allowed to take part in the FA Cup for that season.

History was made on 17 April 1888 when the Football League was officially formed and Accrington FC became one of its founder members, along with Aston Villa, Blackburn Rovers, Bolton Wanderers, Burnley, Derby County, Everton, Notts County, Preston North End, Stoke, West Bromwich Albion and Wolverhampton Wanderers. Representatives from each of these clubs were invited to attend a conference at the *Royal Hotel,* Manchester to arrange fixtures for the coming season 1888-89 and matches were to be played according to the Cup Rules of the Football Association.

The league kicked off on Saturday 8 September 1888 and Accrington lost their first game away to Everton 2-1. Accrington finished their first season in seventh position on twenty points, having won six games, drawn eight and lost eight.

The club remained in the Football League for only five years. In 1892-93, when a Second Division was formed, they spent their only season ever in the First Division, but finished next to the bottom, in fifteenth place. After losing a test match against Sheffield United 1-0, Accrington resigned from the league rather than continue in the Second Division. Financial problems had influenced this decision, so in 1894 Accrington re-applied to join the Football League, but only received seven votes. The club had been unable to pay their rent to the cricket club and were forced to move out in 1894 to a new ground at Moorhead. By now interest was declining and the end of the old Accrington FC was in sight.

The birth of Accrington Stanley
Following their resignation from the Football League, Accrington FC joined the Lancashire League. By 1892 a local team, known as Stanley Villa, believed to have been made up from local players living in the Stanley Street area of the town, was attracting a lot of support and in 1894-95 played in the North East Lancashire Alliance. As Stanley Villa grew and Accrington FC declined, the club eventually took on the town name and became known as 'Accrington Stanley' although for two seasons the clubs played alongside each other at Moorhead.

After the demise of 'Th'Owd Reds', Accrington Stanley moved to Bell's Ground at Woodnook, which they shared with Accrington Villa, another amateur team. By 1894, Accrington Stanley were undoubtedly Accrington's senior football club and in the 1895-96 season they joined the North East Lancashire Combination. In the 1899-1900 season, the club turned semi-professional.

It was around this time that Stanley's president, Captain Harwood, donated, on an annual basis, a set of medals to the non-reserve side

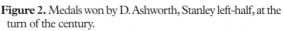

Figure 2. Medals won by D. Ashworth, Stanley left-half, at the turn of the century.
Left: Lancashire Football Combination winners 1902-03.
Right: NE Lancashire Football Combination winners 1899-1900. *Terry Slinger*

which finished highest in the League. Stanley went on to win these on several occasions. At the turn of the century Stanley moved back to their old ground at Moorhead (Figure 1).

In 1901 Stanley were in trouble with the Lancashire Football Association for tampering with the gate receipts from a Junior Cup second round tie. It was proved that £15 19s 0d had been 'improperly retained' and the club and players were suspended until matters were resolved. Eventually four persons were named, suspended from office and the suspension of the club was removed by the Lancashire FA.

This, however, did not affect the team's performances as, in 1902-03, Stanley were in excellent form and went on to win the Combination Championship title, becoming the first non-reserve side to do so, winning Captain Harwood's medals for the first time (Figure 2).

Again in 1905-06 Stanley were Combination Champions and also in that season played Bury in the final of the Lancashire Cup, but were defeated 4-0. At the end of the 1915-16 season, football was suspended until the end of the First World War.

During the early part of 1919 the club was re-formed and, as Moorhead had become too expensive, a dedicated group of supporters got together to buy Peel Park, which was purchased for the club for just £2,500. Originally the pitch ran alongside the school from Manor Street to the *Peel Park Hotel,* but in 1920 it was turned to its new position parallel to Burnley Road. During the next few years, the stand was extended and covered accommodation with new changing rooms erected.

On 31 August 1921 a meeting was held on a lorry in front of the stand at Peel Park at which the club became a limited liability company to be known as 'Accrington Stanley FC (1921) Ltd'. The club was then ready to make its entry into the newly created Division Three North of the Football League.

In the 1920-21 season, which ultimately proved to be Stanley's last season as a non-league club, they won the Lancashire Junior Cup by beating Chorley 2-1 in front of a near 20,000 crowd at Ewood Park (Figure 3).

Figure 3. The team that won the Lancashire Junior Cup beating Chorley 2-1, 29 January 1921. **Left to right**: Pilkington (trainer), Miller, Yates, Pearson, Nelis, Tattersall, Wilson, Stevenson, Caldwell, Quigley, Heslop, unknown, and Smethurst. *Accrington Observer and Times,* 1 February 1921

Stanley's scorers that day were Smethurst and Pearson. Gate receipts for the match were £1,104 18s 9d, a record for the competition at that time.

Stanley in the Football League

History was made on 27 August 1921 when Accrington Stanley played their first ever Football League match in the newly formed Division Three North. Their opponents were Rochdale and the Stanley team was Tattersall, Newton, Baines, Crawshaw, Popplewell, Burkinshaw, Oxley, Makin, Green, Hosker and Hartles. A crowd of 8,500 saw Stanley defeated 6-3 at Rochdale's Spotland Ground. The goalscorers for Stanley were Hosker (2) and Green. A week later

Figure 4. An early match at Peel Park c1921, possibly the first match against Rochdale. Note the away team's transport in the foreground. *Lancashire County Council: Accrington Local Studies Library*

Figure 6. Stanley in action against Blackburn Rovers at Peel Park, 20 January 1937, when they beat Rovers 3-1. *Accrington Observer and Times* 23 January 1937

Figure 5. The team which played against Blackburn Rovers.

Standing, left to right: F. Brennand (trainer), G. Nisbet, J. Craven, W. Gregg, A. Robertson, M. Reeday, H. Andrews, G. Mee.
Front row, left to right, W. Reynolds, W. Rivers, R. Mortimer, G. Pateman (twelfth man), W. Tyson.
Accrington Observer and Times, 16 January 1937

Stanley gained their revenge over Rochdale when they defeated them 4-0 at their first ever home game in the Football League (Figure 4). A crowd of 11,500 was entertained with goals from Makin, Hosker and Green (2). Stanley's biggest win of the season was at home to Durham City in November when they won 5-1. Despite a 6-1 defeat away to Walsall, Stanley had a fairly successful inaugural season by finishing in fifth place with 41 points, having scored 73 goals and conceded 57 in 38 matches.

Stanley's second season in the league welcomed several new players to the club including Andrew Walker, who had played for Chelsea in the 1915 Cup Final and Arthur Metcalf who had playing experience with Sunderland and Liverpool. Stanley finished the season in eighth position with a total of 41 points. Although the team had several good wins that season, including a 5-2 victory away at Ashington and 4-1 home wins over Tranmere, Ashington and Halifax, they had also suffered several heavy defeats, including losing 7-1 away at Grimsby on Christmas Day. Only 59 goals were scored that season with 65 being conceded.

The 1923-24 season saw Stanley finish in thirteenth position, their most notable match being a 5-4 win over Durham City at Peel Park. For the next four seasons, however, Stanley were struggling near the foot of the table, culminating in their worst season to date, when they finished the 1926-27 season next to the bottom in twenty first place. As a result of several heavy defeats, including losing 7-0 away to Nelson and 6-1 away to Bradford, Stanley finished the season with only 27 points from 42 games, having won only ten games all season. Despite disappointing league form, Stanley did reach the fourth round of the FA Cup that season but went out in front of a 30,142 crowd at Stamford Bridge, when Chelsea beat them 7-2, the Stanley goals being scored by Powell and Wyper.

The following season saw an improvement in form with impressive victories of 7-1 and 4-1 over Nelson and a 5-0 win over Crewe. Stanley won eighteen games but lost sixteen and drew eight, which left them in ninth place on 44 points, the highest number they had gained so far. For the next few seasons, Stanley remained in the lower half of the Third Division.

The 1930-31 season was Stanley's worst defensive season so far, when they conceded 108 goals in 42 games, scoring only 84 in reply. Again Stanley suffered several heavy defeats by losing 8-0 to Tranmere, 8-1 to Rotherham and 7-3 at both Carlisle and Chesterfield. Their best win of the season was the return match against Tranmere which they won at Peel Park 5-2.

The Depression of the 1930s affected even football and during this time Stanley were struggling financially; home gates were often down below 2,000 and in 1932 only a bazaar saved them from the verge of collapse. During the 1930s Stanley spent several seasons around mid-table or in the lower half until 1935-36, when they finished in ninth place, their highest league position since 1927-28. They won seventeen games including wins against York 7-2, New Brighton 5-2 and a 6-1 win over Gateshead in which Billy Harker broke the club's individual scoring record by scoring five of the six goals. He was presented with the match ball at the end of the game for scoring four goals in ten minutes.

The following season 1936-37 saw a remarkable victory over Blackburn Rovers in the FA Cup. After beating Wellington Town 3-1 and Tunbridge Wells 1-0 in the first two rounds, Stanley were drawn against Rovers at Ewood Park in the third round (Figure 5). In front of a 31,080 crowd, Stanley held Rovers to a 2-2 draw, both their goals coming from Bob Mortimer. In the replay at Peel Park, a record crowd of 11,636 saw Stanley beat Blackburn Rovers 3-1 after extra time, with two goals coming from Mortimer and one from Walter Rivers (Figure 6). In the fourth round, Stanley were drawn away at Manchester City and before a 39,135 crowd they suffered a 2-0 exit from the FA Cup. Gate receipts from these matches, however, proved a great financial reward to Stanley.

The next two seasons proved disastrous for Stanley as both the 1937-38 and 1938-39 seasons saw them placed at the foot of the Third Division, seeking re-election. At the end of the 1937-38 season, they received 41 votes and were re-elected along with Barrow and the following season saw Stanley re-elected along with Hartlepools United.[1] This last season had seen them gain twenty points and win only seven matches.

The start of the following season began with a complete change of fortune for Stanley who won their first three matches but, unfortunately, when war broke out in September 1939, the Football League suspended matches and did not resume again until 1946-47. During the war years, special war time regionalised leagues were set up and Stanley played in several local leagues until 1942, when they stopped playing altogether. The club re-formed in 1944-45 and the following season saw them win the championship of the Third Division North West Region League.

League matches resumed again after the war and Stanley continued in much the same fashion by finishing the 1946-47 season third from the bottom. Their best match that season was an 8-4 victory over Lincoln at Peel Park in the last match of the season. Stanley's goalscorers were Keeley (2), Smith (2), Edwards and Mercer (3).

The following season saw a great improvement in Stanley's form when they finished the season in sixth place. Notable victories away from home at Carlisle 3-2, Lincoln 3-2 and Rochdale 3-1, and at Peel Park against Stockport 5-2 and New Brighton 5-3, helped them to reach 46 points, scoring 62 goals and conceding 59.

The 1948-49 season saw Stanley finish at the foot of the table again and in spite of finishing in a comfortable thirteenth place the following season, they continued to prop up the foot of the table for the next few seasons. It was during this bleak period that Stanley were to suffer their greatest ever league defeat when, on 3 March 1951, they lost 9-1 away at Lincoln. Around this time Stanley found themselves in financial trouble again and it was only the sale of Stan Lynn to Aston Villa in March 1951 which saved them from going out of existence.

The Galbraith era

The turning point in Stanley's fortunes really came about in June 1953 when Walter Galbraith was appointed player-manager. Under Galbraith things really began to pick up and Stanley finished the 1953-54 season in a respectable fifteenth position, losing only four games at home, with victories including beating Mansfield 5-1 and

Figure 7. The successful Stanley side which finished runners-up in Division Three North, 1954-55.
Left to right (back row): W. Galbraith (manager), J. Harrower, E. Hunter, A. Ashe, T. McQueen, H. Bodle, J. Ryden, C. Sneddon, H. Hubbick (trainer).
Front row: J. Devlin, L. Cocker, G. Stewart, A. Wright, R. Scott. *Garth Dawson*

Workington 4-2. As a result, gates were up to around 8,000 and Stanley played several floodlit games which were also drawing large crowds. During this season Galbraith made several important signings, mainly from Scottish clubs. These included George Stewart and Armour Ashe from St Mirren, Charlie Sneddon from Stenhousemuir, Jimmy Harrower from Third Lanark, Eddie Hunter and Joe Devlin from Falkirk and Tommy McQueen from Queen of the South. Others followed, including John Ryden and later, Bert Scott, both from Alloa, and soon Stanley were fielding a side of almost all Scottish players. The most notable English players at the club at this time were Les Cocker and Harold Bodle.

The following year 1954-55 turned out to be Stanley's best season ever when they finished in second place in Division Three North, their highest ever position (Figure 7). What might have happened had they won the league and promotion into Division Two we will, unfortunately, never know. Stanley finished the season on 61 points, winning 25 games, drawing eleven and losing only ten league matches all season. They scored a total of 96 goals and conceded only 67 in 46 matches. Stanley started the season confidently, but drew their first match at Southport (Figure 8a) and lost their second away at Carlisle. Then came an unbeaten spell of nine matches without defeat, the best being a 4-0 win at home to Oldham followed by a 2-2 draw at Mansfield (Figure 8b). Two defeats followed, Stanley going down 3-2 at home to Barnsley and losing away at Scunthorpe by 4-0. Mid-October to mid-November brought mixed fortunes for Stanley, but a 5-4 win at home to Rochdale at the end of October saw a hat trick for George Stewart, with Les Cocker scoring the other two goals (Figure 8c). A month later Stewart was to increase his goal tally by scoring five of Stanley's six goals in their 6-2 victory over Gateshead at Peel Park. This proved to be the start of another good run for the club, going eleven matches without defeat. On 12 February Stanley lost only their seventh game of the season at Wrexham, on a pitch that was heavily covered with snow.

Between then and Easter, Stanley lost only one more match and so it became vital that they had to do well over the Easter programme if they were to remain at the top of the league. On Good Friday, Stanley were away at York, where a George Stewart goal ensured that they came away with a draw. On Easter Saturday, however, Stanley suffered a shock defeat at home to Hartlepools United when they lost 5-2 in front of a crowd of 11,267 (Figure 8d). Easter Monday saw them drop another point, this time at home to York, when they could only manage a 2-2 draw. In the meantime, Barnsley, their

Figure 8a. This was after the opening match, Stanley v Southport.

Figure 8b. The other side of the fence - Tom Booth's view of the spectators.

Figure 8. The cartoons are the work of a local man Tom Booth, who used the pseudonym 'BEE'. Although one of Stanley's greatest critics, he was also one of their most fervent supporters and his cartoons enlivened the season. The cartoons have all been taken from a sketchbook in the collection at Accrington Local Studies Library which appears to contain rough proofs. Those published in 'The Best Season Ever' are much more polished.

The sketchbook also contains many cartoons by 'MAL', 'NEV' and one by 'Macdonald'. 'MAL' (Malcolm Judge) and 'Macdonald' were both freelance, professional Scottish cartoonists whose work has been published regularly in the *Weekly News* for many years since the Second World War. 'NEV' was Maureen Neville, also a keen Stanley supporter, and obviously a very talented cartoonist herself since her cartoons were drawn when she was only thirteen or fourteen years old.

Lancashire County Council: Accrington Local Studies Library

Figure 8c. Hunting with the Rochdale Hounds.

rivals for the championship, were forging ahead, winning both of their games over the Easter period. The next few matches went fairly successfully for Stanley with three wins, one draw and one defeat, a 6-1 thrashing away at Chesterfield (Figure 8e), taking them to the end of the season on 61 points, four points behind Barnsley and in second place (Figure 8f).

The following year 1955-56 proved to be another successful season for Stanley when they finished in third place. They had only two home defeats, a 1-0 defeat by Grimsby and a 3-1 defeat by York. Their highest score of the season was a 7-0 win at Peel Park against Bradford in September, with goals from Wright (3), Dick (2), Stewart and McCredie. Stanley finished the season on 59 points, winning 25 matches and scoring 92 goals whilst conceding 57. Also during this season, Stanley reached the third round of the FA Cup. Having beaten Wrexham and Darlington in the first two rounds, they were drawn away to Liverpool in the third round (Figure 9). In front of a 48,385 crowd, they were defeated at Anfield 2-0.

Stanley's good run continued throughout the

Figure 8d. The defeat by Hartlepools United was a crushing blow.

Figure 8e. Promotion hopes lost at Chesterfield.

Figure 8f. Almost but not quite.

Figure 9. George Stewart (no 9) tries to win the ball from the Liverpool defence in the FA Cup tie at Anfield, 3 January, 1956. *Garth Dawson*

1957-58 season and again they won 25 games, losing only twelve and drawing the remaining nine games. Following 3-0 wins away at York and Oldham and a 5-2 win at Peel Park against Bradford, Stanley finished the season on 59 points, which was good enough for them to finish runners up to Scunthorpe on 66 points. Sadly, during this season, there was a significant drop in gate receipts. Although Stanley had a successful season, the public of Accrington had not been turning out to watch their team, with gates being down by an average of 1,641 for each home game.

The 1958-59 season saw changes in the organisation of the Football League, when the old Third Divisions North and South were to be replaced by the national Third and Fourth Divisions. Stanley found themselves in the new Third Division, but were they capable of competing with some of the top southern clubs? On the eve of the new season, Stanley received a devastating blow when, following a shareholders meeting in July, the

Figure 10. Peel Park taken from the Coppice, showing the 'Aldershot Tattoo' stand, erected 1958, on the far side of the ground. *Garth Dawson*

chairman, Bob Moore, had accused the Accrington public of not supporting their club, as the previous season had resulted in a deficit of over £4,500. Then, less than 72 hours before the start of the new season, Walter Galbraith resigned as Stanley's manager and Harry Hubbick was appointed to take charge of the team until a new manager, George Eastham, was appointed in October. Ignoring the financial problems, the Board had already given the go ahead for the purchase of a new stand from the Aldershot Tattoo, to be erected on the Burnley Road side of the ground (Figure 10). The cost of the new stand was reported to be in the region of £15,000, an amount the club could ill afford to spend.

Stanley's performances during the 1958-59 season began to deteriorate and they finished the season in nineteenth position in Division Three. With only 42 points from 46 games, Stanley had only managed to win fifteen games. Towards the end of the season came an embarrassing 9-0 defeat away at Tranmere.

In 1959-60, Stanley were to play their last season in the Third Division. Within two years of finishing runners-up, Stanley now found themselves placed firmly at the foot of the Third Division and set for relegation to the Fourth Division. During this season they won only four home matches, their best being a 4-0 win over York. Away from home, things looked even more gloomy. Southend defeated them 6-1 and six teams put four goals past them. Stanley finished the season in bottom place with only 27 points, having won only eleven games and were set for the Fourth Division which was to become their last full season of league football.

Even in the Fourth Division, Stanley found the going tough in the 1960-61 season and could only finish in eighteenth position. A record 9-2 defeat by Crystal Palace and a 4-1 defeat by Mansfield at Peel Park only added to their troubles. With only sixteen wins Stanley had finished the season with a mere 40 points. Added to this was a growing financial crisis at the club, with attendances at home matches barely reaching the 3,000 mark.

The final season
As the 1961-62 season approached, things were not looking good for Stanley, as another financial crisis already seemed to be looming. A bad start to the season left Stanley with only five wins by Christmas, against Darlington, Carlisle, Bradford City, Oldham and Crewe. They had also been knocked out of the FA Cup by Hartlepools United in the second round.

By December the seriousness of the financial situation was

Figure 11. Stanley chairman, Sam Pilkington, being interviewed by a television crew before the last ever home match against Rochdale, 24 February 1962. *Garth Dawson*

realised, when a ban on future transfers was imposed by the Football League because Stanley already owed £3,000 in transfer fees. The Mayor of Accrington, Alderman Wilf Wallwork, immediately launched a 'Save Stanley' Campaign, but with very little success and only £450 was realised, most of this coming from local businessmen.

Throughout January and February 1962, Stanley struggled on

unable to improve their position at the foot of the Fourth Division. On 24 February the club played what was to be their last league game at Peel Park, against Rochdale (Figure 11). The Stanley team that day was: Smith, Forrester, Gregory, Hamilton, Wilson, Cuddihy, Devlin, Bades, Pickup, Ferguson and Mulvey. Stanley started disastrously by giving away a goal after only five minutes and went on to lose the match 2-0. Three days later, Stanley came away from Doncaster with a point after a 1-1 draw in which Mike Ferguson was to score the last ever goal in the Football League for Stanley. The following Saturday, Stanley lost 4-0 away at Crewe in what was to be their last ever league game. The team for that last match was: Smith, Forrester, Gregory, Pickup, Wilson, Hamilton, Devine, Bennett, Smith, Ferguson and Mulvey (Figure 12).

Figure 12. Accrington Stanley FC 1961-62.
Back row left to right: A. Hamilton, W. Smith (player/coach), G. Richardson, M. Pickup, J. Walton. **Middle row:** Mr C.G. Kirby (director), J. Harrower (manager), G. Forrester, A. Smith, P. Vipham, R. Wilson, Mr J. Wigglesworth (secretary), R. Walton (director), H. Hubbick (trainer).
Front row: R. Gordon, L. Bennett, P. Irving, M. Ferguson, D. Sturrock, G. Hudson, P. Mulvey, W. Devine. *Garth Dawson*

As early as 20 February, the Football League had written to the club asking them to clarify their financial situation. Since the club was so heavily in debt, the directors called upon their ex-chairman, Sam Pilkington, for help. He asked for advice from his friend, the Burnley chairman Bob Lord, who agreed to help Stanley but only on condition that the club directors resign and that Sam Pilkington be appointed chairman. Six directors duly resigned but much bad feeling was aroused by the move. Sam Pilkington held discussions with the Football League Secretary, Alan Hardaker, on 23 February and it looked as if the crisis was under control.

On 5 March a meeting of the club's creditors was held and Stanley's financial position was revealed. £43,566 was owing to unsecured creditors, £3,000 was owing in transfer fees and £9,000 was needed to pay the players' wages until their contracts ran out in June. Another £458 was owed to the Ministry of Pensions, although £9,000 was guaranteed by a number of people for the bank overdraft. For the year ending May 1961, there had been a loss of £5,500 and, up to the end of February 1962, further losses amounting to £5,000 were incurred. In all, Stanley owed a total of £62,000. The real blow came when the chairman announced that unless £400 was immediately forthcoming, the telephone, gas, electricity and water would be cut off and the players would not receive their wages.

Realising the seriousness of the situation, Bob Lord withdrew his offer of help and advised Stanley that he could see 'no hope of attempting to carry on'. Within 24 hours, a letter of resignation was on its way to the Football League headquarters. When the players reported for training the following day, they were told that the club had handed in its resignation and that the rest of the season's fixtures had been cancelled.

A last desperate attempt was made to save Stanley when, following a meeting with the club's legal advisers, former director Sir William Cocker issued a statement, saying that the creditors approached had refused to take steps to terminate the club and that several prominent businessmen had offered financial help. He went on to say that, encouraged by this offer, the club had sent a further letter to the Football League wishing to withdraw its resignation.

On 11 March 1962 the Football League Management Committee at St Annes met to consider the matter and, after a long discussion, it was decided that the first letter of resignation should be accepted and so, sadly, Accrington Stanley were no longer a Football League Club. The club's fixtures were expunged which caused some chaos amongst the clubs at the top and bottom of the Division.

Stanley continued to field a team in the Lancashire Combination until January 1966 when the club folded completely ... but not for long, as they re-formed in 1968, joining the Lancashire Combination and now play in the Unibond League. But that's another story!

Further Reading

1. *Accrington Observer and Times*, 1878-1962.
2. Berry, H. *Blackburn Rovers Football Club: a century of soccer*, 1975.
3. *The Best Season Ever: the story of Accrington Stanley Football Club in the season 1954-55*, 1955.
4. Harrison, J. *Accrington Stanley: the story of a Lancashire Football Club*, (Typescript), 1972.
5. Inglis, S. *League Football and the men who made it: the official centenary history of the Football League 1888-1988*, 1988.
6. Jackman, M. & Dykes, G. *Accrington Stanley: a complete record 1894-1962*, 1991.
7. Sutcliffe, C.E. & Hargreaves, F. (comp) *History of the Lancashire Football Association*, 1928.
8. Terry, P. & Ellis, D. *Stanley Centenary: Accrington Stanley Football Club 100 years old 1893-1993*, 1993.

Acknowledgements

I would like to thank the following for their help in supplying photographs and information for this article: the staff in the Local Studies Department of Accrington Library; *Accrington Observer and Times*; Terry Slinger; Garth Dawson. Also thanks to Harold and Ken Harrison for their help with proof reading and computer work.

Notes and References

1 Hartlepools United was formed in 1908 from East and West Hartlepool football teams. The final 's' was dropped to become Hartlepool from 1968-77, at which time 'United' was added again.

10. THE LOYAL TOAST AND ROYAL VISITS

by Helen Barrett

MOST OF US, AT SOME TIME OR OTHER, have raised our glasses and drunk the health of the Queen with the words of the Loyal Toast.

The toast-master makes a request for silence, those present stand and the toast is announced. In the County Palatine, and at gatherings of Lancastrians everywhere in the world, the Queen is, by long tradition, toasted as 'The Queen, Duke of Lancaster'. In 1974 when the boundaries of Lancashire were altered so that the new counties of Greater Manchester and Merseyside could be formed, Her Majesty approved the continued use of the toast by those who wished to use it.

The origins of the title 'Duke of Lancaster' date back to 1362 when the dukedom was conferred on John of Gaunt, but it was George V who requested that the words 'Duke of Lancaster' be added to the toast. In 1913 George V and Queen Mary made a successful tour of Lancashire and, a few days after the conclusion of the tour, Lord Derby received a letter from Lord Stamfordham, the King's private secretary. In it he said that the King hoped that in future, when his health was drunk, the wording of the toast would be 'The King, Duke of Lancaster'.

Whether it was the warmth of the welcome Lancastrians gave to the King which prompted him to make this request is not recorded. For most towns in the county it was the first time a reigning monarch had visited their area and it was an occasion for local people to display their warmth and affection for the sovereign. The visit to Accrington took place on 9 July 1913 during the mayoral year of Captain John Harwood. The formidable task of organising the whole of the tour details fell to Lord Derby, who was also the King and Queen's host at his family seat in Knowsley.

The Mayor appealed to employers to give their workpeople a half-day's holiday and all the cotton mills duly closed at noon. Those fortunate enough to be employed by Messrs Blythe and Company, chemical manufacturers of Church, received a half-day's holiday and a gift of 2/6d.

The royal party arrived via Clayton-le-Moors in a car specially constructed with glass sides. The streets were closed to traffic and

Figure 1. King George V and Queen Mary on the royal stand in Peel Street on 9 July 1913. *Lancashire County Council: Accrington Local Studies Library*

trams on the Baxenden and Clayton routes ceased to operate. It was a splendid occasion. A stand had been constructed on Peel Street, where the King and Queen arrived at 2.30pm. The townspeople packed the street, cheering and waving Union Jacks. Greengrocers did a roaring trade selling orange boxes for people to stand on to get a better view. Among those presented to the royal couple were the Mayor and Mayoress; the Town Clerk and Mrs Aitken; Alderman T.E. Higham and Mrs Higham; Mr Mark Whittaker, the chairman of Clayton-le-Moors Urban District Council; and Mr and Mrs James Cunliffe (Figure 1).

Figure 2. Expectant crowds awaiting the arrival of King George V and Queen Mary at Broad Oak Printworks, decorated in honour of the royal couple's visit 1913. *Lancashire County Council: Accrington Local Studies Library*

Leaving Peel Street, the party made its way to Broad Oak Printworks (Figure 2) where a triumphal arch had been erected. Here local children were accommodated on the sloping ground and each child was presented with a specially printed handkerchief produced by the Calico Printers Association. During a tour of the Broad Oak Works, the King and Queen were invited to try their hand at block printing (Figure 3) and were introduced to Mr Lennox Lee, the chairman of the CPA.

The *Accrington Observer and Times* went to town and produced a special souvenir brochure of photographs of the visit, which was printed by James Broadley on art paper produced by Rishton Paper Mill.

Accrington had to wait until July 1936 for its next royal visit. The Duke of Kent made a tour of the centres founded by Lancashire Social Services to cope with the unemployment crisis. Accompanied by the Earl of Derby and Dr Herbert, the Bishop of Blackburn, the Duke visited the Goodwill Club, which operated in rooms at Union Street Methodist Sunday School, Accrington. In the ladies' section of the club which, as reported in the *Accrington Observer and Times*, resembled a draper's shop, the Duke saw how clothing was made from waste material. He was presented with a woolly green and white suit for his son and, in the men's section, Mr J.H. Butterworth presented a sea-grass stool.

Next the Duke visited the Liberal Club in Oswaldtwistle where the headquarters for women's Social Services was located. Greeted by Councillor Barnes, the chairman of Oswaldtwistle Urban District Council, the Duke met the Reverend and Mrs Dodd and civic

Figure 3. King George V tries his hand at block printing during the tour of Broad Oak Printingworks 1913. *Lancashire County Council: Accrington Local Studies Library*

Figure 4. The royal stand in Peel Street, surrounded by large crowds, this time for the visit of King George VI and Queen Elizabeth on 17 May 1938. There are many enthusiastic flag wavers amongst the excited crowd, including girl guides and boy scouts. *Lancashire County Council: Accrington Local Studies Library*

dignitaries. In the nursery the Duke played with several children and Alice Moores and Agnes Charnock presented toys to the Duke for Prince Edward. At Brookside Mill, the Duke saw how a former derelict mill had been restored to become one of the best Social Services centres in the area.

The Duke took a lively interest in the unemployed people he met and the products they manufactured in the centres so that 'Stella',[1] writing in the *Accrington Observer and Times*, commented on the Duke's charming personality, his slim figure dressed in a black suit and his enthusiastic interest in everybody and everything.

The tradition of a reigning monarch making a country-wide tour had begun with George V in 1913. On 17 May 1938, George VI and Queen Elizabeth followed his example, making a four day visit to Lancashire, and spent all of twelve minutes in Accrington. Accompanied by Lord Derby, the King and Queen arrived at the stand erected on Peel Street, close to Lloyds Bank (Figure 4). A total of 28 representatives of the town's municipal, industrial and social life were presented to the King and Queen. The list included the

Figure 5. Presentation to King George VI and Queen Elizabeth during their visit of 1938. Note the Queen's dress commented on by 'Stella' of the *Accrington Observer and Times.* Lancashire County Council: Accrington Local Studies Library

Mayor and Mayoress, Councillor and Mrs Moorhouse; the Town Clerk, Mr Warhurst; David Bailey, the president of the local branch of the Limbless Ex-Servicemen's Association, some of whose members were also to meet the royal couple; Miss Kenyon of the Accrington Girl Guides Association; Tom Weaver, an employee of the corporation works department; and William Harris, aged 78, the oldest employee at Howard and Bullough's Globe Works.

Junior school children had been given the day off, but the grammar school pupils only half a day. Armed with Union Jacks, the school children who assembled on the Market Ground formed a kaleidoscope of colour. The Queen, who had a reputation for being 'the smiling Duchess', was pronounced to be lovelier than she appeared in the films. The *Observer's* 'Stella', who was renowned for her powers of observation, informed her readers of the Queen's outfit – a grey dress trimmed at the hem with fox fur, a grey straw hat with osprey feathers and grey court shoes (Figure 5).

The presentations complete, the King and Queen shook hands with each of the war veterans on the front row, followed by

Accrington's oldest resident, Mrs Kathleen Barnes. The King and Queen then shook hands, left-handed in girl guide fashion, with Irene Moorhouse, the Mayor's daughter. To the strains of the *National Anthem*, the royal party left for Blackburn, via Church and West End. Twenty five years on since the last visit by a King and Queen, Accrington had demonstrated the loyalty of its citizens.

Less than two months later in July 1938 the Duke of Gloucester, the Duke of Kent's brother, paid an evening visit to the Accrington Lads' Club on Albion Street. His visit coincided with the town's annual holidays but, despite this, he received an enthusiastic welcome. Several of the pylons used to decorate the town at the time of the coronation had been brought out of storage and bunting hung from these at the top of Albion Street. At the club, the Duke was received by the Mayor, Alderman Ellis, and introduced to the president of the Lads' Club, Councillor Alec Higham, who had interrupted his holiday in Bowness to be present. Mr G.F. Bolton, the junior boys' section leader, was introduced as was Mr J. Tustin,

Figure 6. King George VI and Queen Elizabeth arriving at the Howard and Bullough Works on Stevenson Street, Accrington on 8 March 1945.
Left to right: Sir Walter Preston; King George V1; Mr James Redman. Photograph donated to Accrington Library by Mr Ormerod of Accrington 1992. *Lancashire County Council: Accrington Local Studies Library*

the senior boys' leader. The party inspected both the lounge and canteen and watched as twelve year old Alan Foster was instructed in the use of carpentry tools. The Duke also saw the chapel which was equipped with furniture made at London's world-famous Clubland Church, the club founded by the Methodist minister, Reverend Jimmy Butterworth of Green Haworth.[2]

For security reasons, preparations for the next royal visit were, to a great extent, shrouded in mystery. Britain was still at war, but it was fairly widely known that King George VI and Queen Elizabeth were to visit Howard and Bullough's works on 8 March 1945. The King and Queen travelled by road from Burnley and arrived at the Stevenson Street works by way of Blackburn Road and Elizabeth Street. The King, wearing the uniform of Air Chief Marshal of the RAF, was greeted by the Mayor and Mayoress, Councillor and Mrs Slack. The Queen was dressed in a pale blue outfit and 'Stella' even told her readers of the Queen's gossamer silk stockings and grey high-heeled shoes (Figure 6).

Amongst those presented were Norman Entwistle, the superintendent at the Stevenson Street works; John Kirby, employed at the works for 26 years; canteen manageress Mrs Margaret Christian; and Mr J. Jones, an employee for 40 years. Miss Christina Rogan was presented in recognition of the skilled and accurate work she had undertaken as one of the wartime employees. Accompanied by Sir Walter Preston, the president of Textile Machinery Makers Ltd, the royal group toured the works. Noticing four blind men sorting rivets, the King paused for a chat and marvelled at the skills needed to identify each of the rivets. Later the King presented the DFC to Squadron Leader P.A. Rippon, son of Mr A.W. Rippon, the chairman of Textile Machinery Makers Ltd, and a director of Howard and Bullough. Squadron Leader Rippon was himself on the staff prior to joining the RAF. It had been a red-letter day for Howard and Bulloughs and for the people of Accrington.

1953 was a memorable year for Accrington's first lady Mayor, Councillor Mrs Grace Rothwell. In addition to being made Mayor in time for the coronation, Mrs Rothwell welcomed the Duchess of Kent and Princess Alexandra to Accrington in October of that year for a tour organised by the Cotton Board to promote the ailing cotton industry. The visit reminded Accringtonians of the visit in 1936 by the Duchess' husband, the Duke of Kent, who was later tragically killed whilst serving with the RAF during the war. The son of the Lord Derby who had accompanied King George VI in 1938 continued the family tradition of providing accommodation for the royal guests at his Knowsley seat.

In spite of pouring rain, crowds had gathered at Broad Oak Printworks where the visit began. At the Grafton Recreation Club, the Duchess and the Princess met officials of the Cotton Board, the Calico Printers Association and trade union representatives. Mr Herbert Coleman, the Works Manager, guided the royal visitors through the works explaining the various processes. In the screen printing department, the Duchess and her daughter donned protective aprons as they tried their hand at printing handkerchieves as a souvenir of their visit.

A wonderful reception awaited the royal visitors at the Town Hall. The eager crowd, almost 100 *per cent* female, was anxious to see what the Duchess was wearing, since she was acknowledged to be a fashion leader. The onlookers were not disappointed in her grey-green fitted coat, whilst the seventeen year old princess wore a brown coat with a beaver lamb collar. The royal guests lunched in the assembly room with the Mayor and Mayoress, Miss Mary Cocker, after which the guests left to visit Perseverance Mill at Padiham. The Mayor described the visit as the highlight of her year of office and thanked the public for their enthusiastic welcome.

Just ten minutes were allowed on 14 April 1955 for Queen

Figure 7. Presentation of Alderman William Howson to Queen Elizabeth II by the first Catholic mayor for Accrington, Councillor Michael Walsh, 14 April 1955. *Lancashire County Council: Accrington Local Studies Library*

Figure 8. The royal car leaves the Town Hall with Queen Elizabeth II and Prince Philip soon on their way after their fleeting visit in 1955. *Lancashire County Council: Accrington Local Studies Library*

Elizabeth II and Prince Philip to visit Accrington Town Hall. It was a glorious spring day and thousands of people flocked to the town centre to catch a glimpse of their sovereign. Every window overlooking the Town Hall was occupied and the route of the royal car was lined by 8.30am. Five minutes behind schedule, the Queen and the Duke arrived at the red-carpeted portico entrance of the Town Hall to be greeted by Lord Derby; the Mayor, Councillor Michael Walsh; and the Town Clerk, Mr Jack Gartside. Upstairs in the assembly room local dignitaries were waiting to be presented: Mrs Gartside; Miss Higham; Councillor Mrs Rothwell; Alderman Howson (Figure 7); Canon Glyn Jackson; and Father M.J. Walsh.

For all the guests this was the privilege of a lifetime. The Duke enquired where the name of Accrington Stanley originated – Alderman Cocker and Alderman Howson were able to enlighten him! 'Stella' was fortunate to be seated in the assembly room and was struck by the Queen's slight slim figure dressed in a blue fitted coat and blue head-hugging hat. After signing the Distinguished Visitors' Book and autographing large photographs of themselves, the Queen and the Duke descended into the sunshine to be greeted by the cheering crowds. It was then on to Burnley. Accrington's ten minutes of glory were over (Figure 8).

Figure 9. The visit of Diana, Princess of Wales to Joseph Arnold and Co Ltd, Church on 1 June 1983. *Garth Dawson Studio*

The honour of welcoming the next royal visitor to

Figure 10. Foxhill Bank Nature Reserve, Oswaldtwistle taken in November 1987 four years before the Prince's visit. *Lancashire County Council: Accrington Local Studies Library*

Accrington fell to another lady Mayor – Alderman Mrs Haines on 29 November 1958. At Accrington Town Hall, the Princess Royal was received by Lord Clitheroe and introduced to the Mayoress, Mrs Salt; the Town Clerk and his wife, Mr and Mrs Gartside; the Deputy Mayor, Councillor Mr Ridehalgh, and the town's MP Harry Hynd. The prime purpose of the visit was the official opening of St Christopher's Secondary Modern School and to unveil a plaque. The Princess toured the school, meeting the school governors. The school had been completed and opened for its first pupils in September of that year but Mr Killingbeck, the first headmaster, sadly died before the Princess Royal's visit and the school was still without a headmaster.

Almost ten years later, on Thursday 16 May 1968, Queen Elizabeth II paid a short visit to the Dunkenhalgh Hotel, Clayton-le-Moors. It was part of a tour of Lancashire in connection with 'Operation Springclean', a campaign to clean up smoke-blackened public buildings. The road from Rishton was thronged with cheering crowds and many works closed early to enable workers to see the Queen. Lord and Lady Derby accompanied the Queen who was introduced to local civic dignitaries. Mr Arthur Wilson, Town Clerk for Clayton-le-Moors Urban District Council, told the Queen that it was 55 years since a member of the royal family had been to Clayton. Mrs Burrill, the proprietor of the hotel, was presented as were several representatives from 'Padiham Operation Springclean'. Inside the Dunkenhalgh, the Queen signed Clayton's Distinguished Visitors' Book and, on leaving, spoke to several people in the crowd. Whilst the Queen did not visit Accrington itself on this occasion, there was the opportunity to see the royal train pass over the viaduct on its way to Burnley.

The first of June 1983 is a date which will be remembered by many Hyndburn people – for that was when the late Princess Diana visited Church to open the £8 million manufacturing plant of Joseph Arnold's Church Bridge Works (Figure 9). It was a wet and miserable Wednesday afternoon, but the crowds who waited to catch a glimpse of the Princess gave her a heart-warming welcome, showering her with gifts and flowers. The Mayor and Mayoress, Councillor Renshaw and Mrs Renshaw, were presented, along with the Town Clerk, Mr Macgregor, and Mr Frank Kerry, the chairman of Fine Art Developments, the parent company of Joseph Arnolds. Security was tight; police, mounted police and members of the Special Branch mingled with the crowds. The Princess toured the works and spoke to many of the operatives. Susan Smalley of Gloucester Avenue,

Accrington presented a huge greetings card bearing the words 'Australia, New Zealand, the Bahamas... Accrington' with the caption 'You could say she took the pretty route here'.

The last royal visitor to the area was Prince Charles when, on 7 June 1991, he visited Foxhill Bank Nature Reserve in Oswaldtwistle at the invitation of the Lancashire Trust for Nature Conservation. It was literally 'a flying visit' as the Prince landed his helicopter on Harvey Street playing fields! He was introduced to Hyndburn's Mayor, Councillor John Culshaw, and Mr Wedgeworth, the Chief Executive. The Trust's local chairman and site warden, Anthony Flanagan, spent 45 minutes showing the reserve to the Prince who was clearly impressed with the work which had been undertaken on the former tip; he admired the transformation from a derelict and hazardous area to a beauty spot, much of the work done by volunteers (Figure 10).

Times change, things move on, but let us hope that, whoever our next royal visitor may be, our town will be remembered for the warmth of its welcome.

Acknowledgements

I express my gratitude to Lancashire County Council: Accrington Local Studies Library for permission to reproduce nine photographs in this article. I would also like to thank the Garth Dawson Studio for permission to reproduce the photograph of Diana, Princess of Wales.
I should like to thank June Huntingdon for typing this article for me.

Notes and References

1 'Stella' was one of the earliest female reporters on a provincial newspaper, writing before the First World War.
2 James Butterworth, born at Rough Hey, Oswaldtwistle in 1897 into a poor family, became the breadwinner on his father's early death and these formative experiences left him with the desire to provide opportunities for other poor boys to develop their talents and aspirations. He worked towards the foundation of the first Clubland Church opened by Queen Mary on 20 May 1939, a church which included a gym, theatre, art studio and workshops.

11. ACCRINGTON GRAMMAR SCHOOL ACCLAIMED

by Bob Dobson (Pupil No 5723 1952-57)

In the beginning

JUST AS EACH DAY AT ACCRINGTON GRAMMAR SCHOOL commenced with a religious service, in accordance with the law of the land, it could be said that the school itself had a religious aspect to its foundation. For if we look back at the history of secondary education in Accrington, in the beginning there was 'nowt, or next to nowt'. It was only in the 1840s that an educational body arrived through the efforts of Dr Jonathan Bayley, who was minister of the

Figure 1. Mechanics' Institution on the corner of St James' Street and Willow Street with *Willow House* on the site of what is now the public library. The house was the residence of solicitor, James Law, who died in 1858. The Mechanics' Institution was built in 1878 on what was then the garden of *Willow House* and, until it was demolished to make way for the library's opening in January 1908, the house formed part of the Institution. St James' Street used to be a footpath from Union Street to St James' Church known as Woodcock Trees. *Lancashire County Council: Accrington Local Studies Library*

Swedenborgian New Church in Abbey Street during the first half of the nineteenth century. He ran a 'Mutual Improvement Society', the forerunner of the Mechanics' Institution, where young men attended evening classes held in a room in the Sunday School; he also founded the Holland Bank Grove Academy, a going concern by 1844, in which he taught pupils, possibly as a way of augmenting his inadequate salary.

There were others in the blossoming township who recognised this need for 'higher' (rather than elementary) education and they all worked together to establish the Mechanics' Institution in 1845. It started life at 18 Blackburn Road before moving to the new Peel Institution, which was, however, required for a Town Hall in 1878 when Accrington became a borough. The Mechanics' Institution, therefore, removed to a new building on Willow Street at its junction with St James' Street (Figure 1); over a century later in 1989, the first floor of this building again acquired an educational purpose as the only staffed Local Studies Department in the Lancashire County Library service.

It must be realised that the Institution was seen as being for mechanics – ie those involved in the engineering and textile trades of the town for, by educating these people, the lifeblood of the companies employing labour could be protected and their future ensured. Most of the town's elders were connected in some way with its industries and they, together with its ministers of various denominations, were the driving force behind the movement to educate its youngsters and future work force. Initially, the three 'Rs' were the core subjects and sciences and art (drawing) were added later.

Another movement involved in the nineteenth century drive for education was the Accrington and Church Industrial Co-operative Society. That body worked alongside the Mechanics' Institution in providing evening classes and higher grade education and was later to play a part in the foundation of the grammar school.

Long established towns, such as Blackburn, Burnley and Clitheroe, were endowed in Tudor times with grammar schools for their sons (but not daughters), but Accrington had no such institutions. It was a relatively new town with two separate townships, Old and New, until 1878 when the two areas were combined and the resulting borough incorporated. However, as the turn of the century approached and the benefits of education became more widely accepted, the town corporation became wealthier and it was realised that Accrington ought to have an

Figure 2. One of the 'Baltic Fleet' steam trams taken outside the pawnbrokers run by Mrs Hannah Greenhalgh on Infant Street, Accrington 1907. This photograph is a puzzle as there were no tramlines on Infant Street.

Most of the children vying for a place in the snapshot are a little too young to attend the grammar school!

Lancashire County Council: Accrington Local Studies Library

Figure 3. The Technical School, which became the Accrington Grammar School in 1921, around the time this photograph was taken. *Lancashire County Council: Accrington Local Studies Library*

establishment to provide the sort of higher education needed by its next generation of engineers and artisans.

The *Technical Instruction Act* of 1889 enabled local authorities to rate themselves for technical instruction purposes. In the following year the *Local Taxation (Customs and Excise) Act* placed funds at the disposal of councils so they did not face the unpleasant necessity of levying a rate – an extra duty on spirituous liquor paid for this. The Technical Instruction Committee of the council, therefore, decided in 1893 to build a school on what was in reality only a small piece of land, 6,145 square yards, on Blackburn Road, a rapidly growing part of the town. The three storey stone building cost £13,000 to build, of which Accrington Corporation borrowed £10,000. There was a playground but no playing fields for exercise and sport in fresh air. However, there were many who saw the new building as ideal, for all its staff and pupils could either walk to it or be transported on the steam-driven trams which passed by every few minutes (Figure 2).

Accrington Technical School (Figure 3), as it was so named, was officially opened on 28 August 1895 by Alderman Snape, chairman of the Lancashire County Council Technical Instruction Committee. The education bias was – technical. I quote from a contemporary source,

> The main object is to provide complete courses of instruction, especially connected with the industries and occupations of the neighbourhood which the school serves, and by this means afford students a good all-round preparation for their daily work.

The total population of the catchment area for the school in the 1891 census was around 70,000. The total number of all students of whatever age in Accrington was 1,508. Six others attended schools outside the district.

The 1902 *Education Act* formally declared that the town councils were to be recognised as the local education authority – a heavy responsibility but one which was to have enormous benefits to the town in that it enabled the purchase of Spring Hill Council School, followed by others at Hyndburn Park, Peel Park and Woodnook. The Technical School, the only one providing higher education, was controlled by the town as agents of the county.

They're off!

Amongst the first set of 21 pupils at the new school were Oliver Bulleid (Figure 4), fourteen years old, who would become a famous railway engineer; Sarah and Henry Pilkington, the children of a

Figure 4. A group of pupils and staff at the entrance to Accrington Technical School around 1898. The first headmaster, Henry Hills, is sitting in the middle of the back row. Pity the teacher to the left of him with the surname Smirk. Oliver Bulleid, seated front left, became a famous railway engineer; Leo Cheney, seated centre front row, grew up to be a famous pictorial designer. *Author's collection*

Church mill manager of Peel Bank, Church – at thirteen years of age, Sarah was the youngest pupil on the register; Leopold Cheney, fourteen years, a dentist's son, destined to be a famous pictorial designer; Vaughan Sandeman, an accountant's son, who lived at *The Chestnuts*, Church with his cousin Oliver Bulleid. The first pupil listed alphabetically was Stephen Ashton, fourteen years of 379 Blackburn Road. His father was a draper and he became a railway clerk.

The new school's first headmaster was Henry Hills BA, BSc, who came from a senior position at a Dulwich school and was appointed at a salary of £250 per year. The school secretary was John Rhodes, who had made an enormous contribution to the foundation of the school. He had written to Lancashire County Council, reporting the meeting of 19 June 1891 which had proposed a new school, to be called 'Accrington Higher Grade and Technical School', for boys and girls aged ten years and above who had passed an examination. The attendance fee was to be nine pence per week plus three pence for stationery and books. Rhodes was a great force for good in the life of the school. He died whilst still serving in 1911.

Another driving force had been the Town Clerk, Arthur Henry Aitken. He sat with Rhodes and members of the boards of Howard and Bullough, the Accrington and Church Industrial Co-operative Society and the Church and Oswaldtwistle Local Boards to discuss the new school.

The second phase

A girl pupil at the school at this time penned some verses about the school. It began;

> *There is a school in our town*
> *built by the Corporation.*
> *It is a quarter of a mile*
> *From Acc-er-ing-ton Station*
> *And in that school are girls and boys*
> *A credit to the nation*
> *The Head Master is Mister Hills*
> *And he our ev'ry hope fulfills.*
> *The Head Mistress is dear Miss Hodges*
> *And she is up to all our dodges.*
> *The Assistant Head is Mister Court-ice,*
> *And he is considered, by the girls, very nice.*
> *The drill-instructor, tall, erect, stiff,*
> *Is Sergeant Bezzell of the twenty-fifth.*

Henry Hills remained as headmaster for the first four years of the new school's life (Figure 5). He was replaced by Frederick Bastow

Figure 5. Another group of staff and students in the grounds of the Accrington Technical School taken between 1895 and 1898 when Henry Hills, centre with mortar board, was headmaster. Seated immediately to the left of him is Mr Smirk and then Mr Emmott; and to the right Miss Hodges. *Lancashire County Council: Accrington Local Studies Library*

who was to stay for 22 years. Bastow, a tall, lean man, highly respected in the town, developed the social as well as the academic side of the school, introducing Christian socials and literary, debating and dramatic societies.

Another of Bastow's ideas for the development of his pupils was the introduction in 1909 of *The Acorn* (Figure 6), the magazine of the renamed Accrington Municipal Secondary School, which was

> *intended to give an incentive of that pride that we all feel for the old school and will make* (the pupil) *strive to achieve something for the honour of the school, which so largely contributes to the moulding of his character during the most important part of his life.*

It seems likely, however, that the outbreak of the First World War brought about the demise of *The Acorn*.

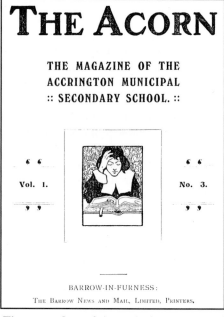

Figure 6. One of the early front covers of *The Acorn*, the magazine of Accrington Grammar School, known then as Accrington Municipal Secondary School, July 1910. The cover was simple but effective. *Lancashire County Council: Accrington Local Studies Library*

In 1911, an Old Students Society was formed. This and its successors of various names was to become a very strong link between the school and its old scholars and the old scholars themselves. I am pleased to say that, although lacking in some formalities, the old boys still dine together twice a year and at least one group of boys who sat and played together in their spring now meet informally once a month in their autumnal years.

In the school's early years, maximum use was made of the facilities in terms of time and space. Evening classes in art, science and technology were held and a School of Art was started under a separate principal, Mr Dawson. This was later to become known as 'The School of Arts and Crafts'. In 1911 Mr Bastow was appointed as Principal and Organiser of Higher Education in the borough as a whole, a sign of satisfaction with his work. When he left in 1920, the day secondary school had 282 boys and 257 girls, a total of 539 pupils. It was said that, 'whether Duke's son or cook's son, they received the same equal treatment from him'.

In his 22 years, Bastow was never absent through illness. A bachelor, he disapproved of boys and girls walking together to and from school and pupils were segregated in assembly. They were marshalled in different corridors prior to assembly and kept separate in classrooms. His pupils, however, liked the old boy – although I suspect that a head having BAST within his name was liable to have his name mis-used! He had an unfortunate glide or cast in one eye so that, when he exclaimed 'That boy over there, stand up!', half the class did so!

Following Bastow's resignation, the corporation advertised his post and received 108 applications. They chose Dr William Catterall Edkins (Figure 7). He was headmaster of a Nottingham School and had previously held the headship at Hindley Grammar School, Wigan. He was a member of the Executive Committee of the Decimal Association. He let it be known that he would be referred to as Doctor C.W. (not W.C. for some reason) Edkins.

Accrington accelerates

A whirlwind had hit Accrington. He kicked the school into action. He shook it by the scruff of its neck. He brought progress. We have Dr Edkins to thank for so many things. He was truly a giant in educational terms. Calling himself Doctor immediately

Figure 7. C.W. Edkins, MA, third headmaster of Accrington Grammar School 1920-1940. *Lancashire County Council: Accrington Local Studies Library*

raised the profile of the school. He set about things with a new broom. He introduced a house system to instil competition – Willows (royal blue), Rhyddings (blue), Coppice (yellow), Clayton (green) and School (red). The house colours (Figure 8) were used as a background on the school cap or bonnet worn by pupils to indicate where their loyalties lay. A member of Coppice House wrote 'We are the house, the others are mere huts' and another sang 'Clayton is the greatest, grandest and most magnificent house' before remarking on

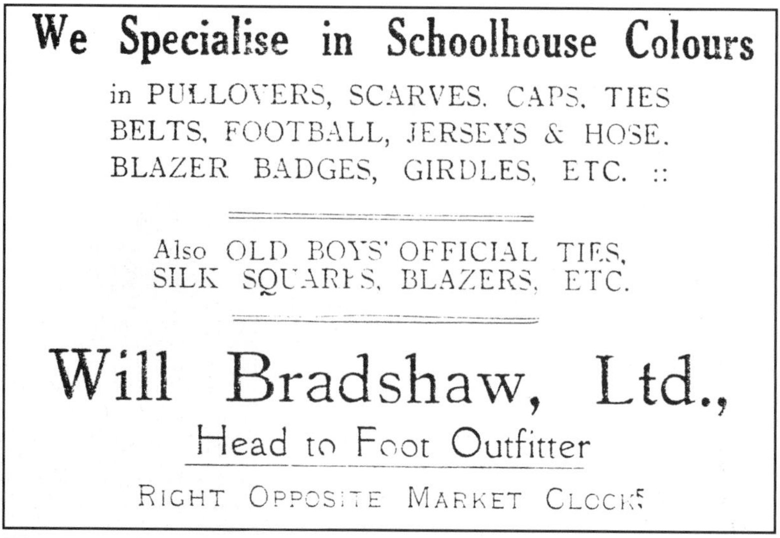

Figure 8. Advertisement from *The Accringtonian* 1933 for school uniforms sold by Will Bradshaw, Outfitter, who specialized in school colours. *Lancashire County Council: Accrington Local Studies Library*

'Weeping Willowsites' (Figure 9). In much later years, School house was to disappear.

Fifty former pupils lost their lives in the Great War. The Old Students Association was inactive during this period until it was

Figure 9. Much later the house system was still in operation. Willows House wins a shield in the summer of 1949. Geoff Walker was House Captain. Do you recognize anyone? If so, please contact Accrington Local Studies Library. *Lancashire County Council: Accrington Local Studies Library*

Figure 10. The official opening of the Parkinson Rock Gardens extension in Oak Hill Park 1933. **Left to right**: Alderman Charles Wilkinson; Henry Parkinson; Councillor Richard Ingham Constantine (Mayor who had become Accrington's first Labour Mayor in 1922); W.H. Warhurst (Town Clerk). In the background is Accrington's War Memorial, described in the last chapter, LEST WE FORGET. *Lancashire County Council: Accrington Local Studies Library*

revived by Edkins, who had by now also given the school its colours - red and black - and started a sixth form divided into A (Arts) and S (Science) classes.

Perhaps Edkins' greatest gift to the 26 year old school came about without any prior publicity in the *Accrington Observer and Times,* nor in the corporation committee minutes. He worked behind the scenes with the result that the Minister of Education wrote to the Mayor of Accrington to say that the school should henceforth be called 'Accrington Grammar School'. Edkins had again raised the school's profile and status. It now ranked alongside Clitheroe, Burnley and Blackburn in the First Division. Those pupils in 1921 must have been bursting with pride as they walked along Blackburn Road.

And there's more

A Speech Prize or Special Day was held in December 1921, the first for many years. Pupils and parents were addressed by Mr Bailey of Lancashire County Council Education Committee, who asked the head for a day's holiday, 'a request which Dr Edkins could not refuse'. That same momentous year, an 'annus mirabilis' for the school, saw the very first Sports Day which lasted until 6.30pm because of the 34 competitive events. E.J. Riley & Co had given a shield for the best sporting house and the Kenyon and Pilkington families, particularly, gave generously in the form of scholarships. Henry Parkinson was also a 'friend and wellwisher'[1] who put his hand in his pocket. His benevolence to the school and the town cannot be over-stated. He is perhaps best known for his endowment of Oak Hill Park with its Parkinson Memorial Rock Garden (Figure 10), but one of his pioneering activities had been to teach technical education to Accrington mill workers from 1881 onwards. He taught cotton spinning and related subjects to workers from Howard and Bullough which resulted in the subsequent establishment of their Technical School.

The school magazine, *The Acorn*, was now restarted as *The Accringtonian* with a new cover at a cost of one shilling for the first 32 page issue. Edkins did not write in it but his influence could still be felt. He made an appeal through the editor for photographs of the 50 lads and lasses who had lost their lives in the war to end all wars. Today's headmasters can teach him nothing.

The school was inspected by His Majesty's Inspector in December 1922. The report stated there were 623 pupils, each paying £6 13 6d per year for tuition from 25 regular and 4 occasional members of staff. The number of pupils had increased from the 262 pupils at the inspection ten years earlier to 418 in 1917 and 557 in 1920. The Inspector commented that 'the most serious feature is the low average leaving age and the short length of school life'. A second staircase was built and the lavatory accommodation extended. Ten years later the Inspector returned to find 626 pupils (335 boys and 291 girls) and a sixth form of 50. The average leaving age had increased along with the duration of school life. The Inspector also found other improvements to praise. 'A sports field and pavilion have been acquired'. The conclusion this time was that the school was

thoroughly efficient, directed wisely with freshness of outlook, and possessed of a vigorous spirit and a highly developed sense of corporate life.

The Accringtonian

Let us look at some of these magazines (Figure 11).

In No 4 (November 1922) someone declared that 'The House of Clayton is now a Mansion, and the "Hut" has been demolished'. By now, boy pupils were going to the town's new swimming baths every Monday and French and Spanish were being taught. The school had a football team of which to be proud.

No 5 (April 1923) reported eighteen boys making a trip to France in the summer holidays. An inter-house tennis competition had been started.

By now, we have noticed that in the magazines, and undoubtedly in school, the christian names of girl pupils were used, but boys were referred to by their surnames.

In No 8 (December 1924) we learn that The Wireless Club, a forerunner of today's Computer Club, had been started.

In No 9 (June 1925) reference is made to *The School Song*, written by Walter Hilton and set to music by Mr Shaw, who had recently left to become headmaster of the new Central School, Oswaldtwistle. There was now a chess club, a sixth form society and a library of sorts. Those leaving school were asked to bequeath a book or a memento

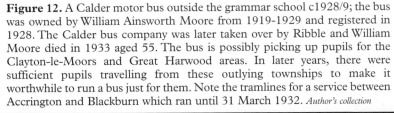

Figure 11. A new name and cover for the school magazine February 1930. Note the letter 'A' on the shield which was replicated in the cap badges. *Lancashire County Council: Accrington Local Studies Library*

Figure 12. A Calder motor bus outside the grammar school c1928/9; the bus was owned by William Ainsworth Moore from 1919-1929 and registered in 1928. The Calder bus company was later taken over by Ribble and William Moore died in 1933 aged 55. The bus is possibly picking up pupils for the Clayton-le-Moors and Great Harwood areas. In later years, there were sufficient pupils travelling from these outlying townships to make it worthwhile to run a bus just for them. Note the tramlines for a service between Accrington and Blackburn which ran until 31 March 1932. *Author's collection*

of his/her chequered career at the grammar school.

No 10 (January 1926) tells us that school had started a week later than usual because of internal painting – something which did not happen frequently, then as now! The new intake did not become first forms; for some unknown reason they entered 3A, B, C or D. The higher forms were numbered 4, Lower 5, 5 and 6. There was also a 'Remove' form in which Latin and Spanish were taught to make provision for late entrants. The Scientific Society heard a lecture from Driver, a sixth-former, on 'the component parts of a wireless set'. It was agreed that the school would benefit from having a wireless set.

In issue No 11 young Leslie Ranson writes on the 1926 General Strike, which had inconvenienced staff and pupils travelling from outlying districts whose transport arrangements (Figure 12) had been disrupted; he later became Mayor of Accrington.

In issue No 15 (December 1928), D. Catlow penned this acrostic:

> *A is for Accrington, where we must swot,*
> *C is for Cramming, the poor scholar's lot;*
> *C is for Chemy., with formulas great,*
> *R is for Reasoning put in one's pate.*
> *I Independence we learn every day,*
> *N is for Needlework taught by Miss K.;*
> *G are the Games which we play with a zest,*
> *T is for Trig., which is rather a pest.*
> *O is the Order in form which we gain,*
> *N are the Noughts which we sometimes obtain.*
>
> *G is for Geomy., Geog. and Gym.,*
> *R are the Ratios, horrid and grim;*
> *A is for Algy, which gives me a pain,*
> *M are the Maths, taught to strengthen one's brain.*
> *M are the Masters and Mistresses, too.*
> *A is Arithmetic, taught by a few:*
> *R are the rest, who are quite a nice crew.*
>
> *S is the System on which the School's run,*
> *C is the Care with which all this is done;*
> *H is the Homework, which is our great bane,*
> *O is the Object we wish to attain.*
> *O are the Obstacles we must make fall,*
> *L stands for Labours, which conquer them all.*

Goodbye Girls!

Since 1895 the school had been co-educational with pupils of both sexes learning side by side. Some differentiation had taken place inasmuch as girls had been taught kitchen and housecraft whereas boys had learned about dovetails and tenon saws. (One teacher of the culinary arts from 1920 to 1939 was the appropriately named Miss Kitchen).

Figure 13. Two school blazer badges. The one on the right succeeded the one on the left, which was also used on the school's stationery. *Lancashire County Council: Accrington Local Studies Library*

Whilst there was not a female head of the school, there was a succession of mistresses who acted as the Head Mistress, a sort of 'Woman Friday', to successive heads to help him understand and tackle the girls' problems. The first of these was Miss Hodges.

Lack of room in the Blackburn Road premises, combined with a desire amongst educationalists and local politicians to provide the best for the town's girls, made a new girls-only school inevitable. In 1939, with Europe already in turmoil, the girls of Accrington Grammar School moved to their new Moorhead home at Accrington High School for Girls, leaving the boys to their own devices.

A changing world

The coming of war in 1939 undoubtedly affected school life. Amongst other aspects, it saw off *The Accringtonian* magazine after 35 issues.

A bombshell was to hit the school the following year when Dr Edkins was replaced by another human dynamo – Bernard Johnson. I like to think there was some wit in the name soon given him by his flock – 'Ben' might be a shortened version of Bernard, but there is also the hidden reference to a great English literary figure.

Ben had held a headship at Barrow-in-Furness following his own education in which he excelled in maths, languages and the great love of his life – music. No boy was in school for long before realising that in each daily assembly, if the songs were not to his liking, the school would hear from

Figure 14. Yet another redesigned cover for *The Accringtonian* December 1950. *Lancashire County Council: Accrington Local Studies Library*

the platform 'Turn back to the hymn' and would be instructed exactly how the tune should and would be sung.

In 1944 the corporation's schools came under the control of Lancashire County Council and it was enacted that 'all pupils are to be educated according to age, aptitude and abilities after an 11 plus examination and prepared for the School Certificate.'

In 1951 'School Certs' were replaced by a General Certificate of Education (GCE) at '0' (Ordinary) and 'A' (Advanced) levels. Until 1955, only grammar school and public school pupils were allowed to take the GCE. We were an elite body.

Ben, noted for the clarity of his mind, had a determination to seek the best for his school and its boys, but he felt the strain of financial strictures in war-time and the post-war period. He had inherited a well-run, proud school but in poor accommodation. A 1948 inspector told of 'narrow, gloomy corridors, semi-basement rooms and the effects of use of the building for evening classes and Art and Technical classes.' The absence of a school library due to lack of space was deplored. The writing was surely on the wall for the school.

In 1950, evidence of Ben's broom came to light. A school uniform was designed and made obligatory, but there was financial help for any family over-burdened by the extra expense. I remember when I first saw the uniform. It was in August 1950, a few weeks before the start of a new term. Brian Jacques, older than I, wore it at our Sunday School but I thought his parents had bought him a replica of the Accrington Cricket Club blazer and cap. It looked far better than the cap with the silver 'A' badge I had seen others wearing over the previous years (Figure 13). The breast badge had a 'fess' or horizontal band in black and was meant to carry any distinguishing marks for prefects, captains or other offices – most lads thought it represented the mucky River Hyndburn. The badge as a whole was reminiscent of the Accrington Corporation coat of arms. A couple of years later, I would be wearing one along with my first wristwatch. No new suit since then has given me quite the same pride in my appearance and achievement. It took a long time for me to forget the fantastic feeling I had when, on Ascension Day 1952, I received a letter saying that I had 'passed my scholarship' and been chosen to go to Accrington Grammar School.

1950 saw the re-emergence of the re-designed school magazine (Figure 14) 'though the paper situation is still murky'. Let us look at some more issues.

1951. School is being repainted for the first time since 1936 – salmon pink walls and sky blue doors! Several 'bop-cuts' were sported by boys in 4C, causing amusement and disgust amongst staff and prefects.

1952. Some boys in 4B wore yellow socks, bop shoes, sleek hair style and flashy American ties 'but not on their way to and from school when blazers and caps will be worn'.

Third year Beverley Rostron took time off from girl-watching and listening to rock records to consider *Our School*.

> *The name of our School is the 'Accrington Grammar',*
> *Standing by the main road, full of beauty and glamour.*
> *It's surrounded by railings all painted in red,*
> *And all boys caught climbing them go to the Head.*
> *Its splendour's increased by a lovely bus-shelter,*
> *Where at quarter to four all the Clayton boys pelter,*
> *Behind is the playground, all tattered and worn,*
> *And in it the cycle-shed standing forlorn,*
> *Inside it is decorated with paint, pink and green,*
> *And from upstairs to down, no more colours are seen.*
> *The best of the rooms are the Office, the Hall,*
> *The Headmaster's study and dark-room so small.*
> *For the rest of our School – it's a babel of noise:*
> *I suppose you all know why – of course, it's the boys!*

1953. A prefect's tie was introduced. Sports Day was held on Church Cricket Field on 20 May 1953. This date may seem unworthy of mention, but it was momentous for me in that it was the first day that I, a tall, gangly second-former just gone twelve, wore long pants for the first time. Some shorter lads only acquired them in the third year.

1955. An election was held to mock the previous week's General Election. Cynicism was rife. The Conservative candidate, Miller, wore a blue rosette and was referred to by Roberton (Communist) as a 'Blackburn Rovers Supporter'. That crack won laughs but not as many as the speech of Whittaker (Independent), then known as 'Wilbur', who later became a professional comedian called Jim Bowen.

Only prefects could join the Yo-Yo Society and only sixth formers could join the Society for the Appreciation of Jazz. A new society was born – The Society for the Appreciation of the Elim Church Posters. An evangelical church had opened almost directly opposite the school gates on Blackburn Road. All good fun. This was the Goon Show era!

1958. Talk of a new school. There were likely to be no ball games after September 1959.

1959. The Head of St Christopher's School allowed our boys changing facilities after games.

1960. A memorial book and bookcase were dedicated to the memory of the 56 former pupils who had died in the Second World War. The cabinet was made by an old boy and another, Rev Furness, conducted the service at a Memorial Lecture night.

Move Ahead

In 1957 Her Majesty's Inspector had again referred to the inadequacies of the building with its small playground of 1700 square yards, inclusive of the bike shed; the playground was used by as many as 450 pupils but ball games were forbidden. Ill-ventilated basement rooms made concentration difficult –

> *kitchen and dining room accommodation is hopelessly inadequate. No showers; only 21 wash-basins with no hot water. The small, badly surfaced playground is rendered less usable during the winter by piles of coke. They have totally inadequate toilet facilities. The time has come when most serious thought should be given to solving this problem.*

Early in 1960, however, the school did acquire a library, long overdue after 65 years, but the following year when Her Majesty's Inspector reported on the new arrival it was concluded that

> *it is not large enough, not used enough and those who administer it are not sufficiently in touch with current thought and practice in the school library world.*

They reported also on the fact that 225 boys, kitchen staff and Art School students took their mid-day meal in two sittings in a room adequate for only 72 people. There had been no canteen facilities at all before Bastow's day when he had arranged the loan of an oven from the local gas and water boards.

The report recommended urgent repairs before re-decoration but held back from enumerating other deficiencies in the premises and equipment because of the possibilities of a new building, concluding that 'with the fresh inspiration of a worthy building, the school's future growth should be healthy'. Were they not aware that the plans for a new school had been struck off the county council's building programme?

The report made for disheartening and depressing reading, although it did end with some praise for the kindly humanity of the headmaster (I found little evidence of that, however, as I bent before him to receive a thwacking across my buttocks!). I thought then that Ben, with his sleek black hair combed across his forehead, had the look of Hitler. As a fifteen year old, I saw him in a different light than I do today. Oh, that I could shake his hand and say 'Thank you, Sir'.

Second-former S. Greenwood penned this verse in the 1961 issue.

> *Grammar School Boys*
> *To see us on our way to school*
> *You'd never dream that we were 'cool'*
> *Our uniforms, so trim and neat,*
> *Make nice old ladies want to weep.*
> *But when at night our homework's done,*
> *And if there's time left for some fun*
> *We wear our 'drains' and chisel toes,*
> *And dash out just to see what goes.*
> *But if you all think that we're mad*
> *(That's the opinion of my dad),*
> *Remember in this age and time*
> *It's hard to dwell on the sublime.*
> *But we'll carry on with our Latin tags,*
> *Our science, maths and schoolboy rags,*
> *And trust we turn out at the last*
> *As good as any in the past.*

A new era

Ben Johnson, headmaster for 26 years, retired in April 1967 and went to live in Hampshire. His replacement was a former pupil of the school from 1940 to 1947, who had distinguished himself in academic and scholastic life after spells in the army and industry. Ralph Bailey, BA returned to the school and brought vigour with him. He had retained a fondness for the school and remembered his time there when the still-serving secretary, Miss Holding, and the janitor, Arthur Street, were younger.

The baton passed to Bailey was a heavy one. He continued to run the school with some changes in staff. Amongst others he lost his deputy and former master, Lou Portno, who had served the school for 40 years. After speaking of 'Pug's' qualities as a teacher – French was his main subject – *The Accringtonian's* editor wrote,

> *perhaps that which will remain most vividly in some boys' memories is his dynamic energy in the pursuit of some offender on the back row when not only the other boys but even the desks got out of his way!*

In March 1968, a farewell evening was held in their 'alma mater' to allow over 500 former pupils – mostly boys – and staff to join together in saying farewell to their building. They sang to Mr Crick's old piano accompaniment; told stories which began 'Do you remember...?'; shook hands with lads they remembered in short pants; then slipped away for a few pints in local hosteleries. They remembered lads unable to be with them. A wonderful evening.

In the previous 73 years, nearly 8,000 boys had passed through AGS – almost 500 had gone to university – and they had been taught by 225 much-loved staff. At 4.00pm on Friday 5 July 1968, the school bell rang for the last time on Blackburn Road. School would reassemble at the new £226,000 building at Moorhead, across the fields from Accrington High School For Girls. My young brother was amongst them. The splendid facilities were state-of-the-art: airy, well-lit classrooms; well-stocked laboratories; a spacious gymnasium; grassy, well-drained sports fields; and, most importantly, the luxury of sufficient toilets. The school was in excellent shape with Ralph Bailey still at the helm.

It is likely that the boys at Moorhead read the *Accrington Observer and Times* or national newspapers and realised there were local and national politicians and some educationalists who were opposed to single-sex grammar schools, regarding them as elitist and unfair. They wanted all boys and girls to have the same education without the stigma of the eleven-plus. They were moving towards what had become known as comprehensive education and this was seen as the way forward. With the hindsight available to the present-day parent, there are many who think that abolishing the grammar school system was not 'forward' at all.

Ralph Bailey kept at work in the early 1970s in a political climate dogged by inflation and economic stringency, keeping his eye on the ball of primary concern – the personal development of his pupils. He continued to value and enjoy the goodwill and fellowship of his staff in the Moorhead community.

Just as Accrington Grammar School was born in a time of educational upheaval, set against a background of political thought and activity, so did it die in July 1975. At that time Ralph Bailey said 'The Grammar School is dead – long live the grammar school tradition'.

Gone but not forgotten
In conclusion I record not only the passing of the soul of the school but also its body. After the 1968 exodus, the Blackburn Road building was retained as an educational establishment, primarily as a satellite campus for Accrington and Rossendale College based in

Sandy Lane. Catering students learned their skills there. On occasion The Old Boys Association held a dinner there, each of them remembering that they were eating in the old 'chemmy' and biology labs.

In 1998, without any prior publicity, the education authority sold the building to a demolition company with permission to demolish. Hyndburn Borough Council officers deserve castigation for not having the forethought to buy back any memento of the building; the gates, gate posts or portico would have made fine exhibits in a public park. Within weeks the slates were off the roof. I received a phone call from a man who had arranged to buy several tons of stone with which to build a house in Wigan. He proposed to place a block on the wall of his house which would read 'ACCRINGTON 1895'.

The newspapers captured the mood of Accringtonians and old boys bemoaning the loss to the town. I wrote to the mayor asking him to try to ensure that whatever was built to replace it, whether a street or a block of houses, it be given a name to associate it with the old school. No acknowledgement. No reply. As I write in July 1999, there is a hole in the ground between Hartmann Street and Lister Street. There is a lump in my throat as I think of it.

In ending my essay I am aware of its shortcomings. There are aspects and facts I have not touched upon, people I have not mentioned. I have over-personalised it. To have been given the opportunity of telling a story previously unrecorded has been a privilege and an honour. There is an extensive archive collection of material in Accrington Local Studies Library (with some similar material for former pupils of Accrington Girls High School). I would urge anyone so minded to take advantage of this wealth of information and write more, especially about some of our Old Boys, famous throughout the country, to heap praise where it is due – on one of Lancashire's finest institutions, Accrington Grammar School.

Acknowledgements

I acknowledge with grateful thanks Lancashire County Council: Accrington Local Studies Library for kind permission to reproduce photographs and extracts from Accrington Grammar School's magazine in this article. I would also like to thank June Huntingdon for all her hard work in typing up this article.

Notes and References

1 Henry Parkinson used the name, 'Accrington Friend and Well-wisher', as a pseudonym to conceal his generous gifts of pictures, photographs, books and other items of local interest to the town. By his death in 1938, he had donated almost 1000 photographs to Oak Hill Park Museum which were later transferred to the Local Studies section of Accrington Library. In 1918 he founded Accrington and District Historical Association. Henry appears again in the next chapter as the uncle of Margaret Jane Parkinson, who married Henry Pilkington, 'an adventurous ancestor'

12. AN ADVENTUROUS ANCESTOR OF MINE: HENRY PILKINGTON OF ACCRINGTON

by June Huntingdon

HAVE YOU EVER WISHED that one of your ancestors had been famous? I did, and much to my delight I found one – well, he certainly led an adventurous life, which is nearly as exciting.

When you enjoy researching family and local history as I do, you find that sometimes information finds you (serendipity in action?) – it is as though your ancestors wish to make their appearance when the time is right. In my case this came in the form of a family bible, which we did not even know existed! A chance advertisement in the magazine of the Lancashire Family History and Heraldry Society stated that a 'Pilkington' bible had been rescued from a dust-bin (literally) and that, if anyone could prove a relationship, they could have it for nothing. As Pilkington is my grandmother's maiden name, I took more notice of the article. Much to my amazement, it had belonged to our Pilkingtons of Accrington! The details (Figure 1) given enabled me to look up old newspaper reports, where... bingo!... I found the story about 'Our Henry' (Figure 2).

Early life

I have Pilkington blood in me, a line which goes back many generations in the history of Accrington. The family lived in the Hollins Lane area of town – *Lane Ends Farm* to be exact.

The farm, long since demolished, was situated almost on the site of the rose garden of Haworth Art Gallery, behind the wall at the junction of Hollins Lane with Newton Drive. Since the national lottery began, I have jokingly said that if ever I won I would love to live on Newton Drive, never knowing, until recently, that my ancestors had lived in that very area.

Henry was the brother of my great-great grandfather David (born 1836). According to newspaper reports written about him, he led a very adventurous life. I often wonder just where all the details came from or how much was travellers' tales, but perhaps I will never know. In any case it makes super reading.

Henry was born in 1829 at *Lane Ends Farm*, Accrington (Figure 3). He began his working life when only seven years old, as a tier boy at Broad Oak Printworks.[1] Whilst still a youngish man, he realised

Figure 1. Extract from the Pilkington family Bible. *Author's collection*

that, if he wanted to get on in this world, he would have to study. He recognised the value of chemistry and he studied this subject at Warren Lane School, Oswaldtwistle. After a few years working at Broad Oak, he chose to leave because of the refusal of the manager to increase his wages by sixpence a week. He now had plans of his own. At that period handloom weaving had not been totally superceded by the power loom and his past knowledge of handloom weavers and their ways became of value to him. He had often observed how the weavers contrived to turn out an excess of cloth and to retain the 'remnants' for their own purposes. Henry purchased these short pieces, bleached them, then printed them as handkerchieves by the block process and sold them. The blocks were purchased from the famous John Mercer of Oakenshaw.

In the 1851 census, Henry was shown as still living at home with his widowed mother, brothers and sisters at Plantation Street, with his occupation shown as 'bleacher'. At a later stage, Henry also manufactured starch. He was not, however, in the 1861 census and was obviously off on his travels by then. At about this time, many printworks' employees from Lancashire were encouraged to go to Scotland. Henry went and became involved in the business of manufacturing the famous Paisley shawls. The Paisley pattern had been widely adopted by the local printworks and was printed on silk or cashmere for the better class trade. A lady wearing one of these, together with a crinoline and poke bonnet, was considered to be in the height of fashion.

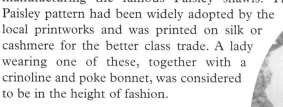

Figure 2. 'Our Henry', Henry Pilkington.
Author's collection
Figure 3. *Lane Ends Farm,* Accrington.
Lancashire County Council: Accrington Local Studies Library

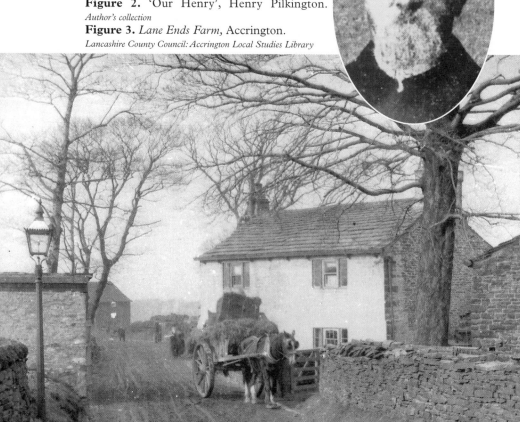

Local newspapers later claim that he went to America in 1854, but the registers show that he married Margaret Parkinson in 1855 at Christ Church, Accrington. On the marriage certificate his occupation is shown as 'shawl printer'. His wife was the niece of Henry Parkinson, the 'Accrington Friend and Well-wisher',[2] and their daughter, Margaret Jane, was born in 1856. Why did he leave a wife and young child? Maybe he intended sending for them at a later date? This could explain why there was a twenty year gap before the birth of his son. Would a wife of today wait twenty years for her husband to return from an adventure abroad? I think not!

Gold digger

The typical Lancashire emigrant to the USA was, generally speaking, from the cotton industry. The practically minded were attracted to the textile towns around Rhode Island or Fall River and New Bedford in Massachusetts. Only those seeking gold or buffalo hides seemed to make for Lowell, a woollen centre, or Minnesota.

Between 1830 and 1930, 40 million people left Europe in search of a better life overseas and Liverpool was one of the main departure points. I think it is fair to assume that Henry also made his way there. Liverpool had well established links with North America, with sailing ships transporting timber and cotton to England and returning home laden with English goods and emigrants. Very few people had a job to go to on arrival. Only a few of the people who went prospecting for gold ever struck it rich, but many secured a reasonable living by farming or working in the towns.

Henry first travelled to Lowell and worked at the Hamilton Printworks there. Whilst he was at Lowell, gold fever broke out. Henry decided to seek his fortune in the gold yielding districts of British Columbia, then a little explored region, chiefly inhabited by Indians. He visited various gold fields and achieved considerable success. He twice made a fortune, but lost it all. On more than one occasion, whilst mining and prospecting for gold, he had his claim 'jumped'. The newspaper article also says he travelled with the Hudson Bay Exploring Party. On one occasion he was shipwrecked, but managed to use a raft to escape. He lost consciousness from exposure in the water and, on regaining his senses, found himself in a hospital. This escapade, however, did not deter him from yet more adventures!

On another 'expedition', he and his party had to find their way through a virgin forest, 100 miles in extent. As a precautionary measure, they chipped marks on the trees and, half way through the forest, they came across Lord Milton[3] and his party, who were lost. Lord Milton, with the aid of the marked trees, was able to find his way out of the 'maze'. Another gentleman whom Henry came across was Lord Strathcona, Governor General of Canada.

During all his adventures, Henry had acquired quite a detailed knowledge of Indian languages and this proved invaluable when he encountered Indians whilst travelling across a prairie. Feeling tired after a long, four day journey, he made a fire and settled down for the night. With his head resting on the ground, he heard in the distance the tramp of horses' hooves and he was very soon surrounded by a tribe of rather frightening looking Indians. He was alone on this occasion and really feared for his life. He asked the Indians the directions to a certain place and was told the distance was 'so many suns'. They became friendly towards him and offered him food and the pipe of peace. They soon departed and in a few hours' time Henry saw a huge fire in the distance. The Indians had set fire to the forest in which they had encamped. Afraid that they would return and attack him, he hastily packed up and started off on his travels again. He walked for three days and three nights before he reached a place of safety.

When setting off on his travels, he would take with him a supply of buffalo beef which had been prepared by dipping in boiling fat and then dried in the sun. According to a newspaper article, we are informed that 'through eating the buffalo beef, his teeth became loosened and he ultimately lost them'. Poor Henry!

During his stay, he became the owner of a large tract of land, on which he had a huge farm. This was near British Columbia and during the American Civil War he was given two alternatives – either to declare himself a citizen of the United States of America or lose the farm. He had no choice – he gave the farm up, reluctantly I imagine, and returned home to Accrington to his wife and daughter.

Back home

He established Pilkington's Soap Works at Commercial Street, Church near the Leeds & Liverpool Canal around 1872. They were the only manufacturers of soap for domestic purposes in the neighbourhood. People may still remember Pilkington's Superior Erasive Soap (Figure 4), Paraffin Dry Soap, Golden Pale etc. They were in large demand and ranked amongst the most popular domestic soaps in the north of England. They also produced a fragrant white 'Windsor' and a very fine 'Old English' dry soap. As the business grew, Henry erected a new factory in Bridge Street,

Church around 1882. He was a director of Messrs Metcalfes of Oswaldtwistle and of Victoria Mills, Accrington where his wife's uncle Henry Parkinson was also a director in later years.

In 1875 his second child, John, was born. Henry was still living in the old family home at 4 Plantation Street, Accrington at this time. His wife, Margaret, was a draper and his daughter, Margaret Jane, was a dressmaker. He eventually moved to Lytham St Annes and then to Thornton Cleveleys where he became a Freemason, being a member of the Leopold Lodge and the Triumph Lodge at Lytham. He was a man of shrewd judgement, a close observer with very practical skills. He rarely drank but occasionally was known to smoke a cigar.

He died aged 86 at his home, *Villa Mar*, Thornton Cleveleys in 1915 and his body was brought home to Accrington by train for burial in the family vault. The cortege, consisting of the hearse and nine coaches, left Accrington railway station and made its way to Burnley Road cemetery. Several of his work people walked alongside the hearse and acted as his bearers and his horse, Titus, was there pulling a private coach.

What an interesting man! I wish I had known him. If I could have a 'One-to-One', I would choose 'Our Henry'.

Figure 4. Advertisement for Pilkington's Erasive Soap discovered by serendipitous chance by one of the editors during the course of working on this book. It was found in a souvenir programme for 1923, *The Marriage Market*, by the Accrington Amateur Operatic Society. *Lancashire County Council: Accrington Local Studies Library*

Notes and References

1 A tier boy (also teer-boy, tire-boy, teering-boy) in calico printing was a boy whose work was to spread a fresh surface of colour on the printer's pad each time he used it. Oxford English Dictionary

2 As indicated in the previous article 'Accrington Grammar School Acclaimed', Henry Parkinson used the name 'Accrington Friend and Wellwisher' as a pseudonym to conceal his generous gifts of pictures, etc to the town.

3 Lord Milton was the title given to a son of Earl Fitzwilliam, but his precise identity is unknown.

13. LEST WE FORGET: THE CIVIC WAR MEMORIALS OF HYNDBURN

by William Turner

A POLITICAL DECISION IN EARLY 1915, that the British war dead were not to be transported home, determined the location and design not only of war cemeteries on the battlefields but also war memorials in Great Britain. The loss of life during the war was on an unprecedented scale. Every community in the country was affected.[1] The families of those killed suffered emotional stress to an unparalleled degree.

After the Armistice, there was a deep need to provide a focus for individual and public grief. The personal and public desire to have a tangible symbol of the mourning for the community's dead resulted in the war memorials one sees in almost every town and village in the country.

Memorials took many and varied forms. They could be anything from a village hall to a book of remembrance, as well as the more familiar civic monument. There was no legislation covering the construction of war memorials; the impetus and methods employed were *ad hoc* and varied from place to place. Some memorials were sited outside churches but always so they could be seen by passers-by; sometimes local land-owners gave land for the purpose; often the memorial was sited on land already regarded as public.[2]

In 1923 a *War Memorials (Local Authorities Powers) Act* enabled 'local authorities under certain circumstances to repair, maintain and protect war memorials vested in them'.[3] This act empowered but did not oblige – Accrington and the surrounding townships which today make up Hyndburn completely fulfilled their responsibilities under the act.

War memorials were designed and built out of strong feelings of pride and sorrow. It was considered important that they were seen as living memorials, eg as the focus of remembrance services. This was to impress on present and future generations the sacrifice and human cost of war. The area which is now Hyndburn more than followed these principles.

A few townships and villages chose the cross, the symbol of hope borne out of suffering; others female figures symbolising faith or victory or peace. The most simple memorial style is the obelisk – an ancient form of commemoration of the dead. It acts as a landmark and can also be enhanced by symbolic figures. Examples of all these can be seen in Hyndburn: Accrington, Great Harwood and Rishton have obelisks; Church, Clayton-le-Moors and Oswaldtwistle chose 'symbolic' memorials; and Altham, Baxenden, Belthorn and Huncoat each decided on a cross. Without exception the money needed was raised by public subscription; even at a time when families had lost their major breadwinner, their generosity was unstinting and collections often consisted of pennies and half-pennies, amounts which, although inconsequential now, would have been difficult to find for many of the bereaved.

Accrington

Accrington War Memorial, in design, scale and situation, is perhaps one of the most impressive in the country. Standing on high ground in Oak Hill Park, off Manchester Road, the memorial is an obelisk in Longridge stone. In front stands a female figure representing 'Compassion and Pity'. On each side of the obelisk are fluted pilasters, bearing tripods from which flames appear, symbolising the spirit animating those who served. The whole

Figure 1. Accrington War Memorial. The unveiling ceremony on 1 July 1922. The first wreath was laid by Captain Harwood who raised the Accrington Pals. *Lancashire County Council: Accrington Local Studies Library*

stands on a massive base on the centre of which is inscribed 'To the honoured memory of the men of Accrington who gave their lives in the Great War 1914-1919'. Below is written 'Their name liveth for evermore.' At the rear is 'This land inviolate, theirs is the glory' and at the lower level is a wall on which twelve Westmorland green slate tablets bear a total of 865 names.

Designed by Professor C.H. Reilly, later to be Emeritus Professor of Architecture at Liverpool University, the memorial was built at a cost of £6,885. An area of land to the west of the memorial was also purchased to ensure that the open view was never obstructed.

A crowd of 15,000 (Figure 1) was present at the ceremony on 1 July 1922, the anniversary of the Battle of the Somme, when the memorial was unveiled by Mr H.H. Bolton JP, a local industrialist and colliery proprietor, whose family had a close connection with the district. Mr Bolton lost three sons in the war and was a generous benefactor to at least three war memorials in Hyndburn.

On 29 September 1951 a second memorial was unveiled for those who died in the 1939-1945 war; a low stone wall in complete harmony with the main structure. The wall bears four green slate panels on which there are 173 names. On a central stone panel appears 'Let us remember those who in their lives fought and died for us'. Inscribed on the edge of the wall is (unusually) 'Northern Ireland' with one name and 'Falklands Campaign 1982' with two names.

In 1922 there was some criticism because the memorial was located well away from the town centre. However, the site was an imaginative choice, overlooking part of the town and seen by travellers to and from the area, whose first glimpse would be an imposing silhouette against the sky. It is an elegant testimony to the men of Accrington who fell in all wars.

Great Harwood

This memorial can be found in Memorial Park set in a Garden of Remembrance, fronting Church Lane and facing Pendle Hill, and was designed and built by Messrs William Kirkpatrick of Manchester.

It is an obelisk in Creetown granite (Figure 2) on the front of which is 'Our Glorious Dead

Figure 2. Great Harwood War Memorial in a lush green setting, August 1998. *Author's collection*

1914-1918, 1939-1945'. A total of 372 names are inscribed around the four sides of the base and on two sides are 55 names of the dead of the 1939-1945 war. At the rear of the obelisk is 'Falklands Campaign' with one name. Inscribed around the base are Laurence Binyon's words from *For the Fallen*, 'at the going down of the sun, and in the morning, we will remember them'.

As early as 18 November 1918, Great Harwood District Council resolved to erect a memorial to the fallen. Subsequently, committees were appointed and public meetings held but none of the ideas for the type and location could be agreed upon. No progress was made until 1925 when a number of ladies, exasperated by the delay and concerned that the town still did not have a memorial, held a public meeting on 5 September. The meeting appointed a Ladies Committee of no less than 65 members. They immediately put forward the idea that a memorial should be erected on land in Church Lane donated by a local man and also agreed to collect money for a memorial fund.

On 2 October 1926 the memorial was unveiled jointly by Major General Sir Neill Malcolm KCB, CB, DSO and Mrs Ormerod of Great Harwood, who had lost three sons in the war. After a short address to the 4,000 attending, Major General Malcolm led Mrs Ormerod to the memorial to pull the cord which lowered the Union Jack covering it.[4]

Figure 3. The original, temporary war memorial at the junction of Blackburn Road and Station Road, Rishton, 1919. *Lancashire County Council: Accrington Local Studies Library*

Figure 4. Unveiling of the addition to Rishton's permanent war memorial to commemorate the Second World War, 7 October 1949. *Lancashire County Council: Accrington Local Studies Library*

The memorial is within a beautifully kept area of lawn and flowerbeds and, although perhaps the least known of Hyndburn's memorials because of its more isolated position, it is one of the most dignified and impressive in the borough.

We owe a lot to the ladies of Great Harwood.

Rishton

Rishton's first war memorial was a temporary structure at the junction of Station Road with Blackburn Road, consisting of a large wooden cross and evergreen plants inside a rectangular base of evergreens (Figure 3). Remembrance Day services were first held there in 1919.

Almost four years later, on 6 October 1923, the present memorial was unveiled. Erected on a triangular site on Blackburn Road, facing The Esplanade, an obelisk atop a pedestal stands on a six-step base. The Creetown granite is embellished with carved laurel wreaths and the whole is surrounded by beautifully kept flower beds and lawns enclosed by cast iron posts and chains.

Over 6,000 people watched as Mrs E. Lewis, who also had lost three sons in the war, unveiled the memorial. Afterwards the 184 names inscribed on the three sides of the pedestal were read out. (Another name was added later). The words 'Pro Patria 1914-1919' are on the face of the obelisk. On the fifth step of the base is a marble scroll bearing the names of the 23 men who died in the 1939-1945 war (Figure 4). An additional name under simply, 'Korea', has also been added.

Rishton's war memorial is impressive in its grandeur and simplicity of design. Although again sited away from the town centre, it is surrounded by well kept houses and gardens. Travellers entering or leaving Rishton clearly see how honourably the town commemorates its dead.

Of the three townships which decided upon symbolic figures, Church chose 'Peace', Clayton-le-Moors 'Faith' and Oswaldtwistle 'Victory'. Therefore, three very different styles arose.

Church

Gatty Park, off Hyndburn Road, can boast a double memorial; a monument and a roll of honour. The monument stands directly in front of Elmfield Hall, which was used as a hospital during the 1914-1918 war but now belongs to Hyndburn Council and is

Figure 5. Church's imposing memorial in Gatty Park in front of Elmfield Hall, September 1998. *Author's collection*

in regular use as a social centre. The memorial is surrounded by a small flowerbed and overlooks a children's play area (Figure 5).

A robed female figure representing 'Peace' is constructed from Portland stone. She stands on a low pedestal, her arms outstretched entreating all to know the sacrifice made by the fallen. On the rear of the pedestal, in the shape of a cross, is the following inscription,

1914-1918

They whom this monument commemorates were numbered amongst those who, at the call of King and Country, left all that was dear to them; endured hardness: faced danger and finally passed out of sight of men by the giving up of their own lives that others might live in freedom. Let those who come after see to it that their names be not forgotten.

1939-1945

The roll of honour inside the hall consists of a bronze panel on which are inscribed 132 names. Two female figures, symbolising the 'Resurrection' and 'Peace', support the panel. The inscription reads 'To the memory of the men of Church who gave their lives for us during the Great War 1914-1918'. The designer of both monument and roll of honour was Walter Marsden, a native of Church, who also designed the war memorials in Bolton and St Annes.

The memorial and roll of honour were both unveiled on 18 September 1923 by Lt Col G.G.H. Bolton MC, the only surviving son of H.H. Bolton JP, who had officiated at the Accrington memorial the previous year. The ceremony ended with a Scottish touch – the playing of the *Piper's Lament* by Accrington Pipe Band.

Clayton-le-Moors

Two figures in bronze, mounted on a square plinth of Portland stone, stand in Mercer Park, near the Church Street entrance. One is an infantryman, the other a robed female symbolising 'Faith'. With one arm round his shoulder she points the other towards France where sacrifice was endured and victory had taken place (Figure 6). On three sides of the plinth are panels inscribed with 225 names, which include two nurses from the Voluntary Aid Detachment.[5] The original bronze panels were later replaced with slate.[6]

Figure 6. An infantryman looking towards France with its suffering, pointed out by 'Faith', on Clayton-le-Moors memorial in Mercer Park. *Lancashire County Council: Accrington Local Studies Library*

The memorial was designed by John Cassidy, also responsible for the Skipton and Stourbridge memorials, and the bronze figures were cast by Messrs Barlanti of London whose firm cast the massive statue of Cecil Rhodes in the Matopo Hills in Southern Rhodesia (now Zimbabwe). It was unveiled on 6 November 1920 by Major General Arthur Solly-Flood CB, CMG, DSO, the former commander of the 42nd (East Lancashire) Division in which so many local men served. The 1939-1945 panel, with 28 names inscribed, was unveiled on 11 December 1949 by Mrs A. Campbell, who had lost two sons in the war. A further name was added after the Korean war.

Flowers surround the base of the memorial and well-kept flowerbeds and lawns with a bowling green nearby make an attractive setting. Everyone entering or leaving the park is able to read the words 'To our glorious dead who fell in two world wars'; 'Their name liveth for evermore'; and also, 'Pass not in sorrow but in lowly pride and strive to live as nobly as they died'.

Oswaldtwistle

Standing at the junction of Rhyddings Street with Union Road, this memorial was unveiled on 14 January 1922 by Major General Shoubridge, the Commanding Officer of the 42nd (East Lancashire) Division, Territorials. Designed by L.F. Roslyn of London, a polished Cornish granite pedestal stands on three steps. On the centre plinth is a bronze pair of soldiers, one of whom is standing and protecting his wounded comrade. From the plinth, project two ship's prows, on each of which stand small bronze figures representing the Royal Navy and the RAF respectively. The whole is crowned by a bronze winged figure of 'Victory and Peace', at whose feet lies a laurel wreath, also indicative of victory (Figure 7). On the pedestal base is inscribed: 'Erected by Public Subscription to the Memory of the Men of this Town who fell in the Great War 1914-1918' and 'Greater love hath no man than this, that he lay down his life for his friends'. On the opposite side there is '1939-1945, To the memory of those who gave their lives in the Second World War' and 'Also those who died in the Korean War 1950-1953'.

In 1922 many in Oswaldtwistle regretted that the names of the fallen were not placed on the memorial. A list of 247 names was published in the local newspaper but no official roll of honour was compiled. The omission of these names (and also those who died in the 1939-1945 and Korean War) makes Oswaldtwistle unique in the Hyndburn group of memorials. Of all the Hyndburn memorials, however, Oswaldtwistle's is probably seen and passed by more people in a day than any

Figure 7. Oswaldtwistle's War Memorial overlooking the busy Union Road. *Lancashire County Council: Accrington Local Studies Library*

Figure 8. The war memorial for Altham is located in the secluded grounds of St James' Parish Church, September 1998. *Author's collection*

other. Its carefully tended site on a busy thoroughfare makes it part of everyday life in the town.

The four smaller villages all chose the Christian cross, the symbol of 'Hope', for their memorial. At the time, 'made to order' memorials were advertised by stonemasons and sculptors. A memorial committee could then choose a design from a catalogue. The advantage, of course, was that the price was within the range of the local population.

Altham

A memorial celtic cross some twelve feet high stands by the lych-gate of the Parish Church of St James. Constructed of polished Cornish granite atop a square pedestal, a sword, signifying sacrifice, is carved on the cross shaft. The inscription 'Our Glorious Dead 1914-1918' is carved on to one side of the pedestal and the dead of the Second World War have been remembered on another side '1939-1945', followed by a further three names. A total of 24 names are inset in lead on all four sides of the pedestal (Figure 8).

The memorial was unveiled on 4 September 1921 by the same Lt Col G.G.H. Bolton MC, 3rd East Lancashire Regiment, who was to perform the same honour for Church two years later. In his speech to the audience of several hundred who attended, Lt Col Bolton 'spoke with considerable emotion' (the names of his three brothers, two killed in Gallipoli, one in France, are on the memorial). After the Bishop of Burnley had dedicated the memorial, the *Last Post* was sounded by two boy scouts.

The *Accrington Observer* commented in its report:

> the most touching part of the ceremony was when the relatives of the fallen placed wreaths at the foot of the cross. Amongst them were a number of little children and none of the spectators could fail to be

affected as they reverently laid their tributes at the base of the monument.

Altham's memorial serves as a reminder of the high price even the smallest of communities paid for the war.

Baxenden

The site of this memorial cross lies just inside the entrance of St John the Baptist's Churchyard, off Manchester Road (Figure 9). Cornish granite appears again in the octagonal base and pedestal atop five steps. A solid piece of granite has been used for the shaft and celtic cross. On the pedestal facing the church is the inscription:

> *This memorial was erected by public subscription to the glory of God and in the memory of our Baxenden lads who gave their lives for us in the Great War 1914-1918. Greater love hath no man than this.*

On the reverse, facing passers-by, is 'In Memory of our Baxenden Lads' and 36 names are inset in lead on the pedestal base.

The memorial costing £450 had been designed by Mr W.J. Newton, Accrington's Borough Surveyor, and the unveiling ceremony on 13 November 1920 was a purely local affair. Official duties were performed by Sir George Bullough, a local industrialist and, in his own words, a 'Baxenden lad' [this is the same George Bullough whose life has been described in Chapter 3. Ed]. The ceremony made more poignant by ceaselessly pouring rain, ended with, unusually for an English village, the playing of the funeral dirge *The Flowers of the Forest* by Pipe Major McDonald of the Accrington Pipe Band.

Figure 9. Another Celtic cross set in churchyard, this time in St John's Parish Church, Baxenden, 1995. *Author's collection*

For almost 50 years, there were no names of those who died in the 1939-1945 war. When this omission was rectified, the inscription was unusual in that the dates given were 1939-1946 in deference to one man who died in Austria in 1946. In November 1994 four names were added.

Although the memorial is within the grounds of the Anglican

Figure 10. Belthorn's memorial cross, September 1998. *Author's collection*

church, it is a village memorial, with a number of Methodists also represented.

Belthorn

Belthorn is just off the B6232 Blackburn to Haslingden Road with the Hyndburn/Blackburn boundary passing through the village. The war memorial at the edge of the village, just inside the Hyndburn boundary, consists of an octagonal column in stone, surmounted by a small covered cross and standing on a base of four steps. It carries the inscription 'Erected by public inscription to the honoured memory of the men of Belthorn who fell in the Great War 1914-1919 AD'. At the rear of the fourth step are four names under '1939-1945' and at the front is 'Falklands 1982' with one name. The total cost of construction was £284.

Major R. Yates RFA, a native of the village, unveiled the memorial on 4 December 1920.[7] He told the crowd of several hundred onlookers that over a hundred men from the district had served in the war and that, of these, 21 had their names inscribed on the memorial.

The memorial occupies a corner site in the centre of a well-kept, walled garden with a wrought iron gate (Figure 10). From a distance the memorial is reminiscent of a French wayside shrine. By the roadside against the gateway is a wooden bench seat dedicated to a member of the Royal Navy who lost his life on *HMS Ardent* in the Falklands.

Huncoat

Erected at a cost of £320, this memorial stands at the edge of a public recreation ground, off Burnley Lane, overlooking Higher Gate Road. A celtic cross of Longridge stone stands on a square pedestal, itself on a base of four steps, with the whole surrounded by a low wall which formerly held iron railings removed in 1939. A gale in 1936

Figure 11. The Huncoat War Memorial. This photograph was probably taken for the unveiling ceremony 29 April 1922 for which the memorial card was produced. *Lancashire County Council: Accrington Local Studies Library*

blew the memorial down damaging the headpiece of the cross and necessitating extensive repairs.

On 29 April 1922 Mr H.H. Bolton, JP proprietor of Huncoat Colliery, unveiled the original memorial in front of a large crowd; nine weeks later he was to repeat this ceremony for the Accrington memorial. The words inscribed on the pedestal were:

> *To Our Glorious Dead. This memorial was erected by public subscription A D 1922 in eternal remembrance of the men of Huncoat who gave their lives for King and Country, 1914-1918. Greater love hath no man than this.*

One of the 25 names on the pedestal is Captain H.H. Bolton, one of the three sons Mr Bolton lost in the war. (His name also appears on the Accrington memorial and, with his two brothers, on the Altham memorial). A stone inset into the second step of the base

HUNCOAT

MEN WHO MADE THE SUPREME SACRIFICE

NUMBER — *Twenty five*

Our Glorious Dead.

bears '1939-1945' and six names.

The knoll on which the memorial stands is 675 feet above sea level, overlooking many square miles of east Lancashire in every direction; a motorway passes nearby. Travellers will never see the inscriptions but all will know it as a war memorial. They will also recognise the perception of those who chose this original and imaginative site (Figure 11).

On 11 November 1920, 'Stella', the Ladies Chain columnist of the *Accrington Observer* wrote

> *During the two minutes silence one recalls the thought of Maurice Maeterlinck – that those who have passed on are dead only so long as they are forgotten by those they left behind. Behind the great silence they live in the land of memory.*[8]

At the turn of the Millennium this is still true.

Further Reading

Borg, A. *War Memorials from Antiquity to the Present,* London, Leo Cooper, 1991.
Boorman, D. *At the Going Down of the Sun: British First World War Memorials,* York, Sessions, 1988.
Boorman, D. *For Your Tomorrow: British Second World War Memorials,* York, Sessions, 1995.
Croad, Stephen *The Conservation of War memorials: Guidance Notes,* Imperial War Museum, 1997.
Darke, J. *The Monument Guide to England and Wales: A National Portrait in Bronze and Stone,* London, Macdonald Illustrated, 1991.
Gregory, Adrian *The Silence of Memory: Armistice Day 1919-1946,* Berg, 1994.
McIntyre, C. *Monuments of War: How to Read a War Memorial,* London, 1990.

Acknowledgements

I acknowledge with grateful thanks Lancashire County Council: Accrington Local Studies Library for kind permission to reproduce six photographs for this article. My thanks are also due to June Huntingdon for her word processing skills in preparing this article for publication.

Notes and References

1 Some three million Britons, ie parents, wives, siblings, children, lost a close relative. In addition, there were other family members who would normally have attended a funeral. Others bereaved were war veterans who had lost comrades in battle. Gregory, Adrian *The silence of memory,* Berg, 1994, p19.
2 Croad, Stephen *The Conservation of War Memorials,* Imperial War Museum, 1997, p5.
3 *Ibid,* p5.
4 It is noteworthy that many names on the memorial are shared by those on the Ladies Committee – no doubt mothers, wives and sisters.
5 Voluntary Aid Detachment – these were members of the local branch of the St John Ambulance Association who volunteered for active service.
6 The panels were stolen in 1971. On the same night similar panels were stolen from the memorials in Helmshore and Whitworth in neighbouring Rossendale.
7 RFA is the abbreviation for the Royal Field Artillery.
8 Maurice Maeterlinck, 1862-1949. A Belgian dramatist, awarded the Nobel Prize for Literature in 1911.

CONTRIBUTORS

1. THROUGH ROSE COLOURED GLASSES: LOOKING AT HUNCOAT

Harold Tootle has always been a keen student of local and social history with a particular interest in the village of Huncoat. On leaving school he started work at Huncoat Colliery but its closure led him to move, along with many other men, to find work in the Nottinghamshire coalfield. With the demise of the coal industry there, he began to study the history of mining and compiled *A History of the British Coal Mining Industry: A Dictionary*, a copy of which is in stock in Accrington Local Studies Library. The dictionary took several years of research and information is still being collected. Several articles and short stories have also been published culminating in the appearance in 1998 of Harry's story of the disaster at Moorfield Colliery on the outskirts of Clayton-le-Moors, *The Moorfield Pit Disaster*.

2. DESPATCHES FROM LOCAL LADS IN THE BOER WAR 1899-1902

Jack Whittaker was born in Haslingden and has lived in this area all his life, moving to Clayton-le-Moors 23 years ago. When browsing through early copies of the local newspaper at Rawtenstall Library, he saw an article about a work colleague of his father. He knew some of the local men who went to serve in the Boer War, both through his father and through his many years with the Church Lads Brigade in Haslingden. This sparked an interest in the subject and he has spent several years researching through the newspapers of Accrington, Rawtenstall, Bacup and Haslingden. He has compiled a detailed collection of transcriptions of these articles, with indexes, to aid other people's research both for genealogy and Boer War history.

3. ROUND THE GLOBE TO RUM: THE BULLOUGHS OF ACCRINGTON

George W. Randall, is a native of Ripon, North Yorkshire and was educated at the local grammar school. He and his wife have lived in Dentdale, Cumbria since 1984. For over 25 years he worked in the agricultural supply industry until being made redundant in 1998. In 1992 he visited the Scottish island of Rum and was immediately captivated by it and its most visible edifice, *Kinloch Castle*. Thwarted in his wish to see inside and unable to find out anything about this late Victorian hunting lodge or the family who built it, he embarked upon his own research and has returned to Rum several times a year since. In 1996 he was the co-founder of the Kinloch Castle Friends Association (KCFA) which is committed to stimulating awareness, care and funding to ensure the continued public availability of this fully furnished period masterpiece. George was a major contributor of text and photographs about *Kinloch Castle* and the Bullough family in *Rum - Nature's Island*, compiled by Magnus Magnusson in 1997. Several of his photographs were included in *Exploring the British Isles - The Highlands and Islands*, Readers Digest, 1998, and *Kinloch Castle: a souvenir booklet*, produced by Scottish Natural Heritage. He is currently writing a definitive history of *Kinloch Castle* and the Bullough family.

4. POSTED IN ACCRINGTON

M.D. Booth studied history at the University College of Chester and, after working as a teacher in Lancashire for 28 years, is now Community Liaison Officer at Oswaldtwistle Mills and Historical Adviser and Education Consultant for the Textile Time Tunnel there. He is presently undertaking freelance work for the Lancashire Museum Service, including the production of educational resources for primary and secondary schools, concentrating on local history in Hyndburn and East Lancashire with an emphasis on the Lancashire textile industry. His publications to date include:

Oswaldtwistle in Times Past; *Woodnook Mills - two centuries of Textile History*; educational resources packs for Oswaldtwistle Mills, Queen Street Mill, Briercliffe and Helmshore Museum. Mike is also occupied with additional contributions to radio, local and family history research and is now working with many others to bring the rich history of the Lancashire Hill Country to the eyes of the world in the new millennium.

5. CANAL WORKERS AND BOATMEN AROUND ACCRINGTON

Mike Clarke has been researching the Leeds & Liverpool Canal for thirty years and has written its definitive history, *The Leeds and Liverpool Canal: A History and Guide*, published in 1990. In the 1970s, he restored and lived on one of the last wooden motor boats on the canal. For many years he was employed as an engineer restoring a wide variety of industrial machinery, from steam engines to textile machinery, from water mills to wooden boats. Today, he is a self employed industrial historian with an international reputation. His current major research project is a history of European waterways.

6. HENRY WATSON (1846-1911): A MUSICAL LIFE

June Tomlinson is a chartered librarian who lives in Accrington and has been employed as a cataloguer at Manchester Central Reference library since 1989. In 1993 she took on specialist duties concerned with the cataloguing of stock for the Henry Watson Music Library. Her serendipitous discovery of Henry Watson's connection with Accrington occurred in 1997 as a result of reading Charles Gidman's pamphlet on the history of St James' Church in Accrington. June has recently achieved a postgraduate diploma in the History of the Manchester Region from Manchester Metropolitan University and hopes eventually to pursue further qualifications in this field. Her immediate plans are to continue tracing her family tree and, of course, that of Henry Watson, about whom there remains much to be discovered.

7. ACCRINGTON NATURALLY

Charles Gidman's interest in natural history began 80 years ago at the age of six with a fascination for pond creatures and caterpillars. His family objected to finding livestock in unexpected places and, when they moved house, he was told they were doing so to keep him away from the pond! On leaving school, Charles entered the textile trade working for the Calico Printers Association in Cheshire, moving to Accrington in 1939. The following year he joined the RAF Coastal Command and on 'demob' took a college course leading to a teaching career, in which he taught at several schools, including St Christopher's. He has also lectured widely on natural history topics. He is a competent musician and artist, exhibiting many watercolours of floral and insect studies in north-east Lancashire. Charles has contributed articles on natural history to various journals and the Nature Notes Column in the *Lancashire Evening Telegraph* in the 1970s. His current project is a series of nature booklets to help raise funds for cancer sufferers.

8. WITH INJUSTICE AND OPPRESSION I MAKE NO COMPROMISE: THE EASTER DUES QUESTION

Catherine Duckworth (nee Mansley) was born in Higher Walton, near Preston, the daughter of a market gardener and a teacher. A great love of reading and a librarian aunt encouraged her to train as a librarian herself. After taking her degree at Leeds, she started work in 1975 at Accrington Reference Library. Her interest in the history of the area was fostered by the enthusiasm of other staff and customers and by the quality of the collection at Accrington. After a career break when her two children were born, she returned to jobshare with *Aspects* contributor, Helen Barrett, both later becoming Local Studies Librarians in the new Local Studies Library. She and her family have lived in the ancient village of Whalley for over twenty years, where she has been active in village and church life. She is interested in her own and her husband's family history and is particularly fascinated with the way the threads of history weave together. This is her first venture into publication.

9. ACCRINGTON STANLEY: A BRIEF HISTORY

Jean Harrison was born in Rossendale and attended Haslingden Grammar School. After leaving school, she worked at Rawtenstall Library before attending Manchester Library School and becoming a chartered librarian. Returning to work at Rawtenstall Library, she held several posts there before moving to Accrington Library, as Lending Librarian, in 1982. Since 1985 Jean has been Branch Librarian at Whalley Library. Interested in local and family history, she is a member of the Lancashire Family History and Heraldry Society. Jean has had two books published: *Roundabout Rawtenstall* and *Vanishing Scenes of the Ribble Valley*. She was also a regular contributor to the now defunct *Red Rose Magazine*. A keen football fan, Jean has followed Accrington Stanley since she was about seven years old, when she remembers paying 6d to go through the turnstiles at Peel Park.

10. THE LOYAL TOAST AND ROYAL VISITS

Helen Barrett considers herself an Accringtonian, having lived here over forty years. Brought up in Haslingden, she was educated at Haslingden Grammar School, Birmingham School of Librarianship and the former Manchester Polytechnic. Following experience at libraries in Burnley, Bury and Wigan, Helen is currently job-sharing the post of Local Studies Librarian at Accrington, where she began her career in 1960, and was a founder member of the Library Association Local Studies Group in 1974. Helen has developed an extensive knowledge of the history of the Hyndburn area, contributing to many local history publications, and her other leisure interests include genealogy and reading. She is currently working on a photographic history of the churches and chapels of Accrington to be published in 2000. She is married to a local businessman and they have one son in his early twenties.

11. ACCRINGTON GRAMMAR SCHOOL ACCLAIMED

Bob Dobson, born and bred in Accrington, now lives near Blackpool but returns every week to his home town. Brought up by his grandmother, Bob was educated at Accrington Grammar School and recalls an interest from an early age in local history, English and Lancashire speech. Following a brief spell in the coal industry, he joined the Lancashire Constabulary in 1960 where he remained until his retirement 30 years later. Bob has written *Policing in Lancashire: A History of the Police Force*, *Lancashire Nicknames and Sayings* and *Concerning Clogs*. He was an officer of the now defunct Lancashire Dialect Society and has edited anthologies of Lancashire dialect poetry. Now a second-hand book-dealer specialising in Lancashire titles, Bob also trades as Landy Publishing, a publisher of local history and poetry books, such as *Accrington Observed*, *Accrington's Changing Face* and *An Accrington Mixture*, which he also compiled and edited. He also writes an occasional column, Dobson's Choice, for the *Accrington Observer and Times.*

12. AN ADVENTUROUS ANCESTOR OF MINE: HENRY PILKINGTON OF ACCRINGTON

June Huntingdon is Accrington born and bred and was educated at Accrington High School for Girls. Her interest in local history began as she listened to tales her uncle, Harry Kay, told of his time serving in the Great War with the Accrington Pals. Having strong ties to a prominent local family, June was inspired to trace her family tree – thus beginning her interest in and passion for genealogy and delving into local history. A member of the Hyndburn Local History Society, June was a founder member of the

Hyndburn Branch of the Lancashire Family History and Heraldry Society and currently holds the position of Publicity Officer. June's specialised subject is circus history and she is also a member of the Romany History Society. At the moment she is researching the transportation of convicts to Australia in the 1800s.

13. LEST WE FORGET: THE CIVIC WAR MEMORIALS OF HYNDBURN

William (Bill) Turner was born in Haslingden in 1931 and is married with one daughter. He left Haslingden Modern School in 1945, but 36 years later he gained an Honours degree with the Open University. After a variety of labouring jobs and two years in the army, he worked in the electricity supply industry as a Principal Assistant in Management Services until his retirement. He has been a Justice of the Peace since 1968. Bill has long been interested in local history. His publications include a book on the hand-loom riots in East Lancashire in 1826 and three books on the Accrington Pals. It is largely due to Bill's interest in and dedication to the Pals' memory that a memorial chapel has been built in St John's Church, Accrington and a memorial sculpture of a broken wall erected on the Somme at Serre. A First World War collection of books and photographs held by the Reference Library, Accrington has also benefited from his enthusiastic support and it has been described as 'the best collection north of Birmingham'.

INDEX

Lack of space has precluded us from indexing all personal names; we have omitted names of footballers and teams other than those in the Hyndburn area, teachers at Accrington Grammar School and many other people and places. Place names relate to Accrington unless stated otherwise.

Figures underlined relate to illustrations.